# GIVE THE CITY
# BACK TO PEOPLE

*New mobility can make our cities a joy again.*

By George W. Jernstedt
with Tom K. Phares

*Published by Cityscope and Mobility Company, 1994*

385.5
J55g

# CONTENTS

University Libraries
Carnegie Mellon University
Pittsburgh PA 15213-3890

# FOREWORD

*By Tom Larson*
*Consultant and Former Federal Highway Administrator*

Some 80 percent of our people live in urban areas. Giving them access to opportunity in a physically and environmentally safe place has got to be one of the central challenges of our time. It's not a new challenge. For as long as people have lived, some dimensions of the current circumstances have pertained. But now there are more people and they are spread over vast areas — areas that are ever-expanding, worldwide. This is a situation crying out for fresh thinking, for innovation.

George W. Jernstedt is a man with fresh ideas. He says in this book that urban transportation should deliver the kind of service provided by the elevator system in a high-rise building — REVOLUTIONARY! Can it be done? This, or something equally creative, **must** be done or our urban-focused civilization is in trouble. Short increments of such service already have demonstrated feasibility.

We now have legislation that requires coming to grips with congestion and clean air, but our tools for doing so are just not up to the job — neither highways nor transit as we know them can do the job. So we come back to Mr. Jernstedt, his Horizontal Development Process and this book. I believe we have here a viable option for improving our urban places — laid out in specific detail and based on years of personal study and experimentation.

This is a book to be read by all those who would grapple with a pre-eminent problem of our people at this time.

*By Kenneth H. Fraelich*
*Executive Vice President*
*Marketing and Strategic Business Development*
*AEG Transportation Systems, Inc.*

W hen George Jernstedt told me he was writing a book capturing his thoughts on people mobility and the Horizontal Development Process, I told him I was anxious to read it, knowing it would include a lot of history related to Westinghouse involvement in the guided ground transportation industry — an industry of which I have been a part for the past 35 years.

George's book did not disappoint me! It is loaded with many colorful, personal stories which I can relate to and appreciate. One was the hectic but ultimately successful development of the BART automatic train control system which established the Westinghouse Transportation Business Unit as an international leader in the industry — a position which continues into the '90s in its new life as a wholly-owned subsidary of the Daimier Benz Group.

While this is not, nor was it intended to be, a history book, the author skillfully uses historical successes and failures to reinforce his central message: the critical need to use the Horizontal Development Process as a basic tool for the planning of people spaces and movement. George Jernstedt has the reputation for being ahead of the industry in many of his concepts on transportation planning. I believe the readers of this book will conclude that the author's ideas on horizontal development can lead to economically solving the future people space and mobility needs, not only for tomorrow, but for today!

*By Walter Kulyk, P.E.*
*Director of Mobility Enhancement*
*Federal Transportation Administration*

T he planning and development of effective public transportation systems in the United States is difficult and complex. The process must involve a host of factors, encompassing technology, design, politics, public policy, administration and management, demographics, land use and funding. Completion of a public transportation system project depends on skillful attention to such factors, while its ultimate success as judged by the riding public depends completely on their successful integration.

Successful transportation investments today are more and more difficult to plan and develop because the riding public is more sophisticated, educated, fiscally conscious, environmentally sensitive, politically active and demanding than ever before. Attention to all of these planning and development factors and their integration is a must.

In this book, George Jernstedt skillfully addresses many of these factors and reminds our planners, engineers, administrators and public officials that they must comprehensively integrate all factors in the planning and development of our transportation systems. He effectively conveys the importance of marrying useful technology with limited funds; of integrating land use with transportation planning; of promoting personal mobility, and making our cities more livable. He urges bringing private developers and their architects into the planning process to benefit not only from their financial resources but from their experience, ideas and demonstrated ingenuity.

Readers will enjoy his historical perspective and conclude that, indeed, we must adopt fresh new ideas in the planning and development of our transportation systems in this country. The health of our cities and enjoyment of our urban environment hangs in the balance.

# INTRODUCTION

P ublic transportation can be exciting and profitable. It can bring people back into the center city and the high density suburbs. This book tells how.

The key is combining far-sighted development with "horizontal elevator" systems. The term horizontal elevator should not be confused with conventional rail rapid transit. It performs on the horizontal plane like elevators in our high-rise buildings perform on the vertical — always available, free and rapid. Such horizontal elevator systems are in daily use in airports around the world and a municipal system exists in the progressive city of Lille, France and in Omiya, Japan.

Horizontal elevator systems will mean the end of conventional transit stations in many cases. Such systems will be absorbed into the buildings of large shopping malls and other commercial development projects. They will take riders right where they want to go — not to isolated transit stations.

Once such easy convenience is available, people again will enjoy our cities and their cultural, commercial and entertainment centers — enjoy them without the hassle of how to get there and how to "get around." With no waiting, no fare collection, no traffic delays, such systems already exist in various cities of the world today, but usually in short increments. They can be applied to whole communities.

The key is to get private development involved. The government's ISTEA program which provides 151 billion dollars for transit over six years is only 50 billion more than is already being invested by private enterprise in projects which include some public mobility, without any real effort to bring the private sector into full participation.

In these pages, the author tells how the technology and methodology for the city of tomorrow was born and is being perfected today...and how it can "Give The City Back To People."

# Mobility, An Ancient Problem Still With Us

"It was now near noon and this was the worst traffic I had ever seen in the city. The vehicles were not even moving. People were pushing and arguing; some of the large vehicles were crossway on the road, trying to go down the center but meeting traffic coming the other way. A few of the smaller vehicles had to pull over to the side to avoid being crushed. From the conversation of the drivers and the pedestrians, this condition happens almost every day — on the Via Appia.

"Suddenly there was a roar of the crowd down the roadway. The guards had made the decision to empty the road of all vehicles. Every cart and wagon was being forced off into the side streets. For the remainder of the day, only people would be permitted on the Via Appia."

This is the way a Senior Roman Guard described a traffic jam on Rome's Appian Way, 1,875 years ago when the vehicles were "wheel to wheel." They had a solution — one we still use today — keep all the traffic off the road when the congestion gets too bad.

There were about one million people in the district of Rome of whom about 90 percent were Roman citizens. But even citizens were subjected to common traffic regulations and had to get off the road at such a time.

Before examining today's situation in our cities to see if we can bring excitement and mobility to public transit, it is worth looking briefly at the early history of man's efforts to achieve public mobility.

It all began when **homo sapiens** 50,000 years ago used only their feet to move about the land. Man's first "transport vehicle" probably was the sled or skid which was invented in several places at about the same time. In Northern China women were used to pull the sleds with thongs.

When in about 3500 B.C. animals first were used to pull the sleds, the donkey was tried on this job. But its obstinacy was recognized early. An ancient mural in Egypt depicts several men tugging at a donkey, front and rear. A third man carries a stick to help persuade the beast to move.

Invention of the wheel was a great milestone. The first wheels were solid round disks. Spoke wheels followed.

In the Tigris-Euphrates Valley lived an amazing people, the Sumerians. Their progress in art, architecture and the wheel surpassed that of all other peoples at the time. First came one-wheeled carts, then two-wheelers, and by 3000 B.C. four-wheeled wagons appeared.

Progress in making wheels spread east and west, reaching what is now Great Britain by 500 B.C., and northern China a short while later. And the wheel brought a most important improvement in mobility — a paved road.

The first paved road probably was in Egypt where a five-eights of a mile stretch was paved from the Nile's highwater mark to the construction site of the Great Pyramid of Cheops. The road took 10 years to build and was 60 feet wide. This may not have been man's first road, since a smaller such project is believed to have been constructed on the island of Cyprus as early as 5500 B.C.

### Mobility and Empires
In 295 B.C., the small city-state of Rome achieved supremacy over all Italy. What was the secret of this success? Mobility — achieved by the Roman Legions through efficient use of roads and wheeled vehicles. Amazingly, some of those roads remain in service even today. Thanks in large measure to the mobility which the Romans created for their legions and their skill in civil government, Roman civilization spread throughout the civilized world of Europe, Britain, North Africa, Egypt, the Middle East, Mesapotamia and Asia Minor. Fifty thousand miles of roads were a major factor in the creation of the Roman Empire.

The importance of the roadway carried on through to the next great empire, Great Britain. The British developed the first turnpike which required payment of a fee for travel on all or a portion of the distance. The year was 1663. Although people strongly objected to this type of development, turnpike construction proceeded throughout England and Scotland. In protest, people actually destroyed some sections of toll roads. Who should finance public mobility was a problem then and it remains a problem today.

Meanwhile in England a new vehicle appeared — the horse-drawn coach. People now were traveling greater distances and wanted to get there faster. In 1706, the trip from London to York took three days. By 1776 this had been cut to 36 hours and within 20 years the coach run required only 20 hours. In those early days of coach travel, London had more than 1,900 coaches plying the streets and there were another 6,000 in the countryside.

### Early City Planning in America

The design of several of America's early cities was influenced by the need for public mobility. There were two great city planners working in America in the early 1700's — the Englishman William Penn and the Frenchman Pierre Charles L'Enfant. Both were widely traveled and familiar with cities abroad. William Penn laid out the city streets of Philadelphia and his plan of the city has survived from 1682 until today with only minor changes. Major L'Enfant, an officer in the French Army, corresponded with Thomas Jefferson after each had visited the other many times. Through their correspondence a planning process was initiated for the Federal City, later to be known as Washington, D.C.

Both Penn and L'Enfant planned for growth. Mobility in their planned cities was high for the first several hundred years. Then came the automobile with its impact on the city. One wonders what would happen if these two city planning pioneers could update their planning for today? We need not just new transit lines or new highways. We need a major upgrading of our entire transit planning. Which brings us to the subject of this book.

It has been well stated by Peter Wolf in his book "The Future Of The City," when he says:

"Transportation has always influenced city location, city form, in fact the destiny of cities. The impact of the wagon, the barge, the ship, even the railroad are minor compared to the complex, multifaceted influence of the automobile on the evolution and development of cities. In the beginning of this century, when the car was introduced to city streets, it was seen as a dramatic and joyful toy celebrated by most advanced thinkers as a step forward, one that would make the city all the more delightful and available. We now know, after a brief but bewildering experience, that the automobile is able to severely diminish the experience of the individual in the city and to create a pattern of cityless, region-wide habitation never before experienced in the history of man."

The automobile has led to a phenomenon of this regional growth which, of late, has been called the "Edge City." Really a "non-city," the Edge City is a high density suburban pattern of growth which has occurred out on the edge of the big cities but has not been created by any common master planning process. Each Edge City is different according to area market demands and none is a real city in the sense of being a multi-functional community.

A common danger of these Edge Cities is that they depend almost entirely on the automobile, largely because highway funding is so available. We must beware of any such syndrome which limits mobility to the automobile, severely restricts pedestrian mobility and depends largely for its functions on high rise buildings. More about these matters of city growth and mobility later.

The city can be a **laboratory**. From it we must learn the lessons of good and poor mobility. Our vehicles, great as they are, limit their own growth by the success they temporarily enjoy. Each vehicle, each component, each mode has its day in history. The sled, the wheel which has spawned many types of vehicles are seeing new equivalents appearing as air support, magnetic suspension and other forms.

But we have become bound by our conventional practices — highway, transit, street patterns and pedestrianism. Our planning has become a cooperative exercise — a process of compromise — not an integrated process. We must do a better job of planning for integrated, horizontal growth.

This book will, I hope, make the case for the need to plan not primarily for cars, buses, trains and planes, **but for people**, in creating greater public mobility in our urban areas. The secret, if there is one, is the intelligent integration of improved transit technology with the exciting new methods and forms of urban development.

Tomorrow's city will be a wonderful place.

# CHAPTER ONE

# More and More Cars, Less and Less Mobility

As I walked down the steps of the transit station, I faced a row of what looked like glass elevator doors. But through the glass I could see a transit vehicle coming into the station. A "horizontal elevator." Behind a big window at the front of the transit car sat two children pretending to drive the car. They were having a ball. There was no operator!

Tears came to my eyes. This was an automated transit system developed in my hometown of Pittsburgh 20 years earlier by a team of Westinghouse engineers under my management. That pioneering system had been rejected by the local politicians as unsafe, "ahead of its time," largely because there was no operator and because some key local leaders had little vision for the future. Here in the early 1980's was that same system operating routinely in Lille, France, a city the size of Pittsburgh.

When this transit car stopped, the people seemed to flow on and off with no delays at all. How come? Suddenly I noticed that nobody was collecting tickets or fares. I timed the interval to the next vehicle arriving. 55 seconds. What mobility!

How this came about is the story of automated rapid transit integrated with private development — a story still unfolding in our cities. That story is part of the struggle to free our urban centers from the paralysis of traffic congestion and municipal debt. It is a struggle to give Americans real urban mobility at a profit.

This is not a story about conventional mass transit. It is a story about how to make it possible for people to move easily and conveniently within the developments and functional locales of the city. It is about people not vehicles.

Actually, it is two stories in one. First, the story of how to accomplish the improvement of mobility or people in the city, and, second, the story of mobility of information. The flow of information is vital to progress in mobility improvement. Too often we use a crutch — political compromise — to substitute for a free information flow. Compromise assures maintenance of the status quo. It conceals leadership and achievement.

Changes in methods often are controlled more by how the information is handled than by the merits of new technology.

### I Love My Automobile. . . Except
First, as a former president was fond of saying, let me make one thing perfectly clear. Because I seek to end traffic congestion in our cities, doesn't mean I am out to eliminate the automobile!

Being **for** more urban mobility doesn't mean being **against** the automobile. I love my automobile. A great invention. It's ready to go when I am. It goes right where I want to go, even stopping on the way if I have to pick up a package. It's comfortable — just marvelous transportation.

Except. . . it's taking longer and longer to get to my destination. And when I get there I wish my car would disappear because too often there is no place to put it.

Except. . . the automobile is pushing some of our big cities such as Los Angeles to the upper limits of air pollution due to fumes from the millions of internal combustion engines. The Clean Air Act Amendments of 1990 and 1992 will severely limit or shut down auto traffic in these center cities by 1995 if they fail to take meaningful action.

But will I give up my car for city driving? Not until I get something better!

And that's the problem that's facing our urban areas. That darling of American transportation, the automobile, is leading our congested cities toward traffic gridlock and pollution paralysis. And the "something better" — which ought to be some form of public transit — continues to be largely ignored or drowned in red ink.

It's not that we haven't seen this problem coming.

As new highways and streets began to pour more and more vehicles into our cities in the years after World War II, city planners and transportation engineers looked to the future with growing concern. Many envisioned the day when traffic congestion could destroy the economic viability of our cities, make our industries non-competitive in the world and pose a threat to our environment. Acres and acres of valuable land in our cities were being inefficiently used as we attempted to cope with the transportation needs of expanding urban areas. Higher and higher office towers were rising like weeds in the field. The city was becoming a commercial oasis. But room for people and people activities was disappearing.

Beginning in the 1960s, there was a great deal of talk about this. Countless conferences and seminars were held. Plans were proposed and legislation enacted. First results came in the form of major highway projects, foremost of which was the national interstate highway program. But public transit for our cities stayed on its nostalgic and traditional course as states and municipalities set out to keep alive or expand existing bus systems and conventional subway and street car systems.

### Needed: Some New Ideas
What was badly needed at this point were some new ideas, some daring, some excitement to give public transit a shot in the arm. And, indeed, some new ideas were tried. In Western Pennsylvania, Allegheny County's Port Authority built and successfully tested the world's first automated (no operator) transit system. An exciting idea!

Visitors from around the world came to see, learn and copy. But this pioneer "Early Action Program" became caught up in the fierce cross-fire of Pittsburgh politics. "Ahead of its time," cried the old-line politicians, and the County backed off. Instead, it built a circa 1930 trolley system, streamlined and called by the new name: Light Rail Vehicle. More about this unfortunate bit of history a little later.

While the U.S. took a hesitant and fragmented approach, we watched other nations making progress. High-speed trains for intercity travel appeared in Japan and then France. The automated transit technology, rejected in Pittsburgh, surfaced successfully in those countries. The Japanese and French copied it down to the last semiconductor, and even improved it.

I had many interesting experiences riding these new systems and meeting the people who were pleased and delighted with their progress. Today they're selling their improved systems back to us. But they deserve credit for their initiative, not criticism from those in America who dragged their feet.

Meanwhile, in the U.S., public transportation remained stagnant. The **hard core urban transit problem** — moving people from the burgeoning suburbs where they now live into the crowded cities where they still work — **resisted solution.** And intercity public transportation could boast of but one significant advance — the relatively slow "high-speed" New York-Washington Metroliner trains.

"Why won't people get out of their cars and ride public transportation?" wailed dozens of governors, mayors, city managers and transportation "experts."

I have probed this question for more than 25 years, traveling hundreds of thousands of miles to study the relationship of transit with commercial development in scores of cities throughout the world. And, along the way, I've directed advanced transit projects. As a result, I believe I've come to understand the problems and what it takes to solve them. Some answers have become clear — answers that give hope for success in moving people with much greater efficiency in the decades ahead.

There is ample technology available. The need for better transportation is there. Urban and suburban development is going strong. The future can be exciting. But transportation gridlock can keep it from happening unless we get our act together and do it now! We must remember that the mission is not only to make it possible for people to get to the center city, but also to make them **want to come.** Public transit must appeal not only to commuters going to and from work, but also to those who chose to come into town for shopping and entertainment and the other "people activities."

Why hasn't this happened before now? More than 25 years of exposure and investigation into this question have produced this answer. For too long we have kept our eye "on the track" as it were — on trains or trolleys that ran on rails and stopped at stations — and produced deficits in the process. Or bus systems that followed the same paths with the same results. The basic planning process used 60 years ago in the 1930s is being followed still today. And that must change.

### The Essential Elements
If we assume that improving the mobility of the American people is both desirable and do-able, we must recognize the need for concerted action dedicated to that goal. Drawing on my own experience, I believe four elements are essential to reaching this objective.

(1) We must have **vision.** Research and development now at our disposal can provide us with the ability to restore our urban centers through the implemen-

tation of new and advanced transportation systems — outside the hard shell of public transit bureaucracy. However, new technology should be used only when it improves mobility and not merely to demonstrate engineering achievement. **We should not build new high speed systems until we have provided our urban centers with greater access for public transit to feed and load these systems.**

High speed rail or magnetic levitation systems will not find a market unless our urban centers have transit systems that will provide or accommodate their passengers. We must stretch our imaginations and reach beyond mere expansions of existing technology to create integrated systems — systems that not only will move large numbers of people efficiently and comfortably within our cities, but will also provide essential people-friendly activities within the system.

(2) We must have strong **private sector involvement.** I am convinced that public transit needs a "heart transplant." Its heart until now has been reliance on government funding and centralized direction which continues to just "look down the track." Its heart in the future must be reliance on private funding and commercial development.

Public agencies and political management have performed poorly on their own. Achievement has been found largely in the private sector. It is time to let private business into the transportation arena. Greater participation by private developers and entrepreneurs is essential, not just through assessments or funding but through developers designing, constructing, managing and operating transit systems or segments of systems.

Over the past two decades, the innovative transit ideas have come from individual private developers — men like John Portman (glass elevators), Walt Disney (monorail right into the hotel lobby) and Leigh Fisher (10 horizontal elevators at Tampa International Airport).

(3) We must have **improved worldwide communications** on transportation developments. All of us must obtain a better understanding of how the flow of information both within our country and abroad can speed or block progress. And we must plan accordingly. Without improved direct communication among the transportation authorities, state and municipal bodies and qualified private developers and architects, we will neither learn from our failures nor benefit from our successes. Our planners and political leaders must be informed, for example, about what a system like the one in Lille has accomplished for that city.

As part of this communication we must **audit performance** to avoid transplanting unsuccessful operations from city to city. As it is now, failures at home often are reported "out of town" as successes, for political reasons. Two of our last center city automated transit systems are failures but have not been so reported by their operators. Independent auditing is one of the keys to success in the financial world. It must be used in the field of public transit.

(4) We must have **coordinated planning**. America has been the victim of terribly fragmented planning during the past 25 years. What is needed is recognition that increments of a transportation and development network must work together from a business standpoint. First we must improve mobility **within** our cities, with interested public and private input to meet the varying local requirements. Then we can work on improving movement **between** cities. But local planning efforts must be done within a framework that recognizes the ultimate goal of interregional, intermodal linkages.

Up to now, highway authorities have pushed highway improvement. Rail authorities have pushed rail development. Urban authorities have called for better mass transit, but can't agree how to do it. Our comprehensive multimodal planning just combines separately planned systems. If we were to plan our vertical buildings like we have been planning horizontal expansion, adding transit systems to our cities might look like Fig. lA. This sketch is an exaggeration, of course, but schematically is quite close to the truth. By comparison, the vertical building design of the Hotel Regency in Atlanta provides greater mobility and higher patronage (Fig. lB). Unfortunately, new methods and new technology have been orphaned or left to domestic equipment manufacturers. These domestic manufacturers, in turn, have become discouraged and have been deserting the transit business.

The comprehensive planning process must be upgraded to handle increased numbers of people — not only their vehicles — in the center city.

Government has given only lip service to participation by the private sector, while continuing to extract additional fees or taxes. Government has considered the role of the private sector simply to hand out money. Private developers have not been brought into transit planning as full participants although they have ideas, initiative and financial resources that are going unused. It is they who have provided the most exciting developments of the past 20 years — the shopping malls and tall building complexes. Public transit has experienced little such excitement, just a repeat of the past.

It is possible today to build fast, convenient, low-cost and appealing forms of transportation integrated with people activities — forms of transportation and development that the public will patronize and which provide a service that the public will demand. In some places, it's already being done. In Lille, France and Kobe, Japan fully automated transit systems have been integrated in new town developments.

What is happening in such enlightened systems is the disappearance of the conventional transit station. "People activities" — shops, restaurants, hotels, theaters, offices — stand right at the doors of the transit vehicle. The secret ingredient that makes possible such people-oriented development is the willingness of private developers to provide transit to and from their facilities, doing so at a profit to themselves and at a saving to the taxpayer.

Don't get the idea that the future discourages our love affair with the automobile. Let me say again that the automobile is the finest individual transportation system in the world. But we must help it out, improve its performance and give it the proper place in the total transportation network.

Where the auto gets in trouble is in our urban and suburban high-density population centers. The key to solving these problems will be found not only in the use of new mass transportation technology, but in development of user-friendly **people-transit interface**. The conventional "transit station," as we know it, is obsolete. We don't need horizontal transit stations any more than we need vertical elevator stations. The interface between people and transit must be an integral part of project development.

Public transit systems that supply only a commuter-type service are enormously expensive due to heavy equipment requirements and empty return trips. In the past, we have been expecting transit lines to stimulate commercial development. But it has to be the other way around. Commercial development must help **create demand** for transportation. We will only solve the problem of cost and of ridership when we give the customer a transit service that meets his needs.

Why haven't we done it already? Lack of vision, poor communication, uncoordinated and fragmented planning which isolates and insulates private development, all must share the blame.

### Vision Plus Communication
Speaking of the need for vision and communication, a few remarkable people have vision and are just naturally open to new ideas. They love 'em. Walt Disney was such a man. And he was a great communicator.

I first met him through my company's district manager in Southern California, Jack Boggess, who was responsible for doing business with Disneyland. Having dealt with Walt on numerous occasions, Jack knew that Disney had some imaginative ideas about moving people and felt that he and I should talk. So we invited Disney to visit our experimental automated transit project in Pittsburgh and ride the so-called "Skybus."

Disney came, he rode the automated system and he loved it. He invited me to visit California and discuss with his organization new ideas for moving people in the planned Walt Disney World.

So it was that my family and I headed for California to get acquainted with Disneyland. On arriving, we took the monorail from the parking lot to the station opposite the hotel. Of course, we had to carry our bags down the stairs and across the street. I thought, why do we have to do this?

I met Disney the next day out in back of WED Enterprises where he had built a long wooden structure for testing a new loading platform to be used in his transportation exhibit at Disney World. He opened our conversation by kidding me about Federal money being used to pay for my test track in Pittsburgh, pointing out that his test equipment was all paid for by his private earnings.

I allowed as how he probably got more Federal funding than I did as a result of his 55 percent tax credit. He laughed and said he would have to agree. Then I brought up the subject of our monorail ride from the Disneyland parking lot.

"Do it differently at Disney World," I suggested. "Bring the transit vehicles right into the hotel lobby. Don't make your guests get off across the street."

Walt liked the idea immediately and asked for sketches. I gave him the sketch (Fig. 2A) to indicate how to design the inside of his Contemporary Hotel. The lobby and monorail vehicles were integrated with all the hotel services. Walt was pleased with the sketch and said that's how the hotel would be designed. (Fig. 2B) shows how true he was to his word. You get off right inside the hotel lobby. Even the outside of the building (Fig. 2C) is much more dramatic when exciting changes are done well.

That idea was accepted easily and Disney followed it completely — no jealousy about pride of authorship. But you're not always working with a Walt Disney.

Walt asked for ideas for his EPCOT development, too. This second theme park adjoining the Magic Kingdom at Walt Disney World was to be a showplace for my new horizontal development transit ideas. Sadly, however, Walt's death intervened and the new management changed EPCOT (Engineered Prototype of the Community of Tomorrow) to mainly an international exhibition area featuring various foreign countries. EPCOT is indeed a financial success. But the original experimental community or "new town" idea, as well as my opportunity for participation, were lost.

### How Ideas Travel

That often happens to new ideas. Few of us in the transportation arena have the good fortune to work with a Walt Disney. I've found during my career that there are four principal ways that important information moves. It can be bought, borrowed, given away or stolen. And sometimes it suffers the worst fate of all. It can be **ignored**, particularly in high places where it's urgently needed in decision-making. That has been the fate of many key ideas in the field of transportation.

But you can't keep good ideas bottled up for long. There are very few secrets anymore in the world of technology. In America, we don't live in a goldfish bowl — we live in a sieve. Important technical information leaks out like flour being sifted!

The Germans, Japanese, French and other countries have a standard procedure for procuring patent copies, technical articles and any information available on what we are doing with new products or processes. They often have patent information even before it is officially issued by our government.

They study it carefully. And they obtain sample products or material early in the manufacturing process — legally or otherwise.

Other nations certainly know the importance of information flow. The outside world studies everything America does, good or bad. They copy, improve and even sell it back to us. That's the way the Japanese got their early lead in such things as high-speed rail, electronic equipment, cameras and computers. That's the way the French got their lead in nuclear power plants with Westinghouse pressurized water reactor technology.

Making it easier for our foreign competitors, much of America's technical information we don't even try to protect. We sell it, or give it away. That's what happened to the automated guideway transit (AGT) technology in the 1960s. Information flowed freely from Pittsburgh to transit experts of many nations — at our own initiative. Since it was partially funded by the U.S. Government, we had to give it away.

When Westinghouse and Allegheny County's Port Authority were running the new, fully automated system on a test track in Pittsburgh's South Park in the early 1960s — an experiment which, for the first time, completely eliminated the operator in a rapid transit system — a steady stream of foreign experts visited the site. Since direct labor is a tremendous expense in a transit system, these foreign observers sucked up all the information we could give them — voluminous detailed reports, photographs, everything. It was all free! They not only copied our system, but they improved on it. Westinghouse was required to make the information available since the Federal Government furnished about half the funding. But could we get such information for similar projects in Japan or Europe? No way!

Today representatives from those same countries are sending in their marketing people, **selling** U.S. cities and airports the technology we **gave away**. France, for example, sold its automated transit system — patterned after the pioneering Pittsburgh system —to Chicago's O'Hare Airport and the City of Jacksonville, Florida. We helped make information flow in all directions! And it's coming right back home "under new management!"

# CHAPTER TWO

# An Early Try For Mobility, The Trolley Car

If you are old enough to remember the 1920s or 30s, you probably have a nostalgic love for the trolley car. It may have taken you and your first date to the movies. It took the crowd "out to the ball game." It was Mother and Dad's way of getting to town to shop or work.

Before the horseless carriage took over our city streets, the trolley was the way to go. It was America's first real effort to bring mobility into the city.

What happened to this noisy, rattling old friend that we used to depend on for mobility? Has it gone the way of the one-horse shay and disappeared entirely?

No, but it sure has changed. And its offspring is writing a new chapter in public transportation.

The trolley had humble beginnings. It started as a horse-drawn car pulled along iron rails. But it didn't really become popular until the age of electricity. Electric trolley cars first appeared on city streets only several years after London and New York began to supply electricity from Thomas Edison's first central electric generating stations in 1882.

These trolleys were primitive critters indeed. Their iron underframes were supported by two axles with rigidly mounted wheels driven by electric motors. Because the wheels couldn't turn right or left, the trolleys couldn't be longer than about 20 feet.

It was in 1888 that Frank J. Sprague devised and successfully installed in Richmond, Virginia what could be considered the first electric trolley car line. Looking at its primitive deficiencies, it is difficult to understand how people loved this early trolley. But progress was coming.

In 1897, a new trolley was introduced in Manchester, N.H. with a swiveling, two-axle undercarriage that helped eliminate derailments. And soon thereafter, a trolley with two swiveling trucks permitted the car to go around sharp curves. The trolley grew to 50 feet in length and found increasing use as a mode of interurban travel when roads between nearby cities were still largely rough and unpaved.

By the time of America's entry into World War I in 1917, there were reported to be 18,000 interurban trolleys and a total of 45,000 trolley cars, all electric. This clean and relatively efficient mode of transit is credited with playing a major role in starting the migration of people to the suburbs.

The early trolley car not only had efficiency going for it. It was fun! Some trolleys in the late 1800s had a parlor car (Fig. 3A). In Montreal, a Golden Chariot was operated on recreational runs (Fig. 3B). The trolley seemed to have a personality of its own as it impacted the lives of the entire family. For summertime, it could be boarded from either side along the full length of the car (Fig. 3C). Customized models appeared such as open air cars for sightseeing. So it became popular for many types of excursions. Naturally, London insisted on double deckers (Fig. 3D).

Use of the trolley spread up and down the east coast and then jumped to the west coast where it spawned the cable car — a San Francisco institution still today.

I can still hear the clang-clang of the trolley as I rode every day in the early 30s from Bloomfield, N.J. to Newark to attend classes at the Newark College of Engineering. Some of those same cars still are in use today on a private right-of-way into the city as part of a subway system.

Over 50 years of daily use. What a record!

### The PCC Car
The 1930s saw more improvements in the trolley car. Recognizing that they were heavy, uncomfortable and slow when compared with their new rival the automobile, the industry made a major thrust to revitalize them. They organized a Railway Presidents' Conference Committee in 1931 to design a new and better trolley car.

The Committee did a good job. Great technical improvement was accomplished which made the new PCC cars high performance, high-speed vehicles. They were an early example of standardization. The first 20 were delivered in 1934 to Washington, D.C. to impress the nation's capital. My hometown of Pittsburgh received the first generally supplied cars in 1936.

These trolleys were much quieter and ran more smoothly than their predecessors. The body was made of pressed steel with roof, sides and underframe welded to form one structure. It was mounted on double trucks in which rubber was inserted at all moving joints, replacing steel springs.

The new cars moved faster and were more comfortable. Four motors were geared flexibly to each axle to drive the cars at speeds up to 45 m.p.h. New braking assured smooth stops. And forced ventilation drew fresh air through ducts in the roof to relieve the old stuffiness — "air conditioning" circa 1934.

The PCC cars not only were more efficient and comfortable, they cost less, thanks to one standardized design.

### The Trolley's Decline

For a short time, the transit industry feasted on this sudden progress, manufacturing more than 2,000 cars. But then the city trolley and interurban systems started to decline. One reason, of course, was the rapid rise in use of the automobile and the development of street and highway systems. America's romance with the automobile was coming into full bloom. But the second reason was not as obvious.

The auto industry and its suppliers wanted no competition from street railways. General Motors and Standard Oil of California started to buy up the trolley systems and replace them with diesel buses. Most of the 80,000 electric street cars of the 1920s were gone by the start of World War II. They were sold to other countries, principally in South America where several hundred still are running in Argentina, Brazil and Venezuela. As spare parts are needed, they simply take another car out of service and "canabalize" it.

The most devasting move was the gradual buyout of the $100 million Pacific Electric System lines and equipment all around Los Angeles. It was accomplished by a combine of GM, Standard Oil, Firestone Tire and others.

This was the beginning of LA's air pollution problem as the burgeoning automobile and bus traffic spewed its fumes into the skies. It still is doing so today. The loss of the private rights-of-way that disappeared in this move will hurt the Los Angeles commuter for years to come, because any successful transit system depends for top performance on separated rights-of-way.

By 1949, GM had been involved in the replacement of more than 100 electric trolley systems with GM diesel buses in 45 cities including New York, Chicago, Philadelphia, Detroit, St. Louis, Baltimore and, of course, Los Angeles.

In April, 1949, a Federal jury in Chicago convicted GM of having conspired with Standard Oil of California, Firestone and others to replace electric transportation with diesel buses. The penalty? The court imposed a $5,000 fine on GM and convicted one of its executives. He was fined $1.

The eruption of World War II also helped bring famine to the electric street railway industry, of course, as the manufacture of such vehicles was halted to give way to defense production. No more PCC cars ever were built and no further improvements would be made in the trolley car for the next 40 years.

At this point, the trolley's performance problems lay not so much in the trolley car itself, but rather where it ran — down the center of the street. It had to empty its passengers right into the path of traffic alongside. To try and solve this problem, "safety zones" were built in the streets at busy Intersections, and the motor bus became the alternative method of public transit.

Beginning in 1928, a new trolley had been created to help solve this middle-of-the-street limitation. Some cities tried combining the trolley and the motor bus, creating an electric "trolley bus" that could pull over to the curb. It could still make contact with the overhead electric wires by means of a flexible swivel connection for the trolley poles on the roof.

The trolley bus was swift and quiet, but it still lacked desired flexibility and it increased total costs. So it slowly yielded to the gas or diesel-fueled motor buses whose fumes increasingly make our cities smell like Kuwait City after Operation Desert Storm.

But the trolley car in America wasn't finished. New ideas began to surface in the 1960s as city officials struggled against overwhelming traffic congestion. They began to hear ideas like separate rights-of-way, tunneling, automated control, high-speed rail and the lure of Federal funds.

Like most new ideas, these new advances in transit technology and methodology encountered bitter opposition from the old line trolley buffs and hide-bound politicians whose nostalgia and resistance to change overcame their judgment.

I did make one effort to initiate a trolley automation project in the early 1960s with my firm's local competitor, Westinghouse Air Brake Company (WABCO). But WABCO was uneasy about the Westinghouse work on our newly designed and totally automated transit system and refused to cooperate on trolley automation. Too bad. The trolley car had a lot more life in it, having its separate rights-of-way.

Loss of people mobility in our cities has been caused by many things. One of the mistakes was to eliminate the trolley car before there existed a worthy successor.

Happily, the worthy successor to the trolley — automated and on its separate right-of-way — now is emerging as one of the heroes in the fight for mobility and integrated people developments.

# CHAPTER THREE

# America's Slow Start on Mass Transit

When I first poked my head into the world of mass transportation in the late 1950s and early '60s, all automotive transportation projects were in the Highway Department. Mass transit issues were in the Department of Housing and Urban Development (HUD). We were playing around with a lot of mediocre plans with an old-fashioned Bureau of Public Roads. There was one fine exception, however — the Interstate Highway system.

Across the Pacific, Japan was gearing up for a new kind of war — a commercial war. Electronics was the first battlefield and transportation was the second. I'm sure other battle grounds lay ahead. We see evidence of it today. Medicines, small appliances and other products are coming to our shores.

The war left the American people with a different mind set than the Japanese. We were getting ready to sample the pleasures and benefits of the peace — automobile trips, new family homes and new household gadgets. We could hardly wait to enjoy life a little.

The Japanese people had their minds on a different set of values. They wanted to make up for all the time lost in the futile war. They went to work and to school, requiring no coaching to get their act together. They wanted to win the next competitive test.

One of the fields in which Japan benefited from this group effort was public transit, both at home and in exported products.

With government help, Japan built its New Tokaido line between Tokyo and Osaka over which the "bullet trains" raced at 150 miles an hour. Today it's part of the privately-owned Japan Railways.

I was to benefit from inside involvement with the people who designed and built this line, thanks to a post-war arrangement which Westinghouse had with its Japanese licensee, Mitsubishi.

Every two years a new Japanese family would move into Wilkinsburg, a Pittsburgh suburb, for training at the big Westinghouse plant nearby in East Pittsburgh. The father would be a young Mitsubishi engineer. Inevitably, the family felt very alone in this foreign country and my wife and I tried to be of assistance to them in shopping, school and home life.

One such family in 1948 was that of Takeo Kato. His specialty was transportation, and we did many things together. But after his two-year assignment in the U.S. ended, I saw no more of him until 20 years later.

It was in 1968 when I was responsible for our Mitsubishi license and was visiting Tokyo that I had a phone call from Kato. It took me a moment to remember who he was. Then I recalled his stay with us two decades before. He told me he had a luncheon arranged in my honor the next day. I turned from the phone to check my schedule with my Japanese host, a Mitsubishi vice president, who said that luncheon the next day would be impossible. Prior arrangements interfered.

Mr. Kato asked to speak with my host. When the Mitsubishi VP got off the phone, he said we indeed would be going to lunch with Mr. Kato tomorrow. I inquired who Mr. Kato was and was told he now was president of a large Mitsubishi subsidiary and was on the Board of Directors. What a long way from that training assignment in East Pittsburgh 20 years before!

"I do what he tells me to do," said my host.

At the luncheon the next day I was seated alongside a very quiet gentleman with graying hair who Mr. Kato introduced as Dr. Hideo Shima. Mr. Kato explained that Dr. Shima had built the high speed New Takaido railroad which featured the famous "bullet trains." This was a man honored by all nations.

Mr. Kato did not quit. He informed me that Dr. Shima would retire from the Japanese National Railroad the next day. I turned and congratulated Dr. Shima.

Mr. Kato still did not quit. "You should hire him to help you in your country," he said, quite firmly.

Without hesitation, I did just that. Then Mr. Kato relaxed.

I later found out that Japanese people follow an old custom. When a person does something very good for you or your family, it is considered to be an "ON." Such a kindness must be repaid sometime in your lifetime.

So it was that Dr. Shima and his wife spent several months with us in America and our families have exchanged visits numerous times over the years. Our most recent visit was from two granddaughters of Dr. Shima. This friendship with the Shima family has given us much joy and enlightenment. I often think how much Americans could learn by befriending our Japanese neighbors instead of being critical of their success.

Dr. Shima's contribution to Westinghouse business certainly illustrates this. At the time of his original visit, we were competing for contracts to build equipment for the Metroliners — high speed trains that were to run between Washington, D.C. and New York — and I hoped the man who had made the bullet trains work so well could also put us on the right track.

One thing we were working on was a new motor for the Metroliners. So was GE. Both companies were spending several million dollars on the new motor project. After studying what we were doing, Dr. Shima asked me if I knew anything about the motors he used on the New Tokaido bullet trains.

Then he stuck the knife in.

"They're motors designed by Westinghouse at East Pittsburgh in 1933," he said. "They are very reliable and require very little maintenance."

Instead of using our old motors like the Japanese were doing, we were designing new ones at great cost because we believed they were necessary to handle anticipated 150 mile-an-hour speeds.

So much for new technology. This postscript might be added: the new Metroliner motors that we and GE were working on never were successful. They had trouble at the low operating speeds at which they were run. The Metroliners never could reach their 150 mph designed speed because of the poor roadbed.

That's what Dr. Shima talked about when he turned to engineering .

On the top of the Metroliner cars would be those frame-like devices called "pantographs" that reach up and make contact with the electric wires overhead, called "cantenaries." That's how the train gets its electric power. The pantographs are flexible so they can increase or decrease their "reach" (travel) as the track level varies due to variation in the height of the roadbed.

Dr. Shima asked how much the travel of the pantographs on these trains would have to change on the Washington - New York run. We made an investigation and found they would have to extend their travel from 16 to as much as 22 feet, depending on the roadbed, the bridges and tunnels.

Then he dropped the bombshell.

"Between Tokyo and Osaka," he said, "this distance varies from its regular 16-foot travel by plus or minus one centimeter — temperature compensated." His pantographs hardly ever move, which permits very high speed and the brushes last a long time.

This, he quietly reminded us, is not research. It's just good engineering. And, he added, unless that roadbed was rebuilt, the U.S. Metroliners would never be able to approach the speeds of the Japanese bullet trains. Where were the government consultants who designed the Metroliner system? Why did two large American companies like Westinghouse and GE bid on the project? Embarrassing questions.

The Metroliners today run occasionally at about 110 miles per hour for short sections of the run. In Japan, the New Tokaido line increased its top speed in 1990 from 150 to about 180 mph., and started to expand the system (Fig. 4A). We will talk more about high speed trains in Chapter 12.

Japan organizes for large projects to make sure information flows even to competing firms working on parallel projects. It's in Japan's interest for that to happen. Japan has few restrictions on how companies can work together, unlike the U.S. On those bullet train motors, for example, Mitsubishi had a license from Westinghouse to produce them, but the Japanese government said Mitsubishi had to share its production with another Japanese company. Westinghouse received royalties from Mitsubishi but not from the second supplier. In fact, Westinghouse people weren't even allowed to visit the other supplier! Had that other supplier made a manufacturing improvement I don't think we ever would have heard about it. The flow of information was blocked at that point.

Today, a Japanese consortium has been established called HMT — Hitachi, Mitsubishi and Toshiba — that works on jobs requiring the best combination of experience and capability of each company. Similar cooperation also exists in Europe and is particularly effective in large projects. Suppliers learn about the benefits of coordinated effort in other ways — all of which benefits the customer. U.S. antitrust laws prohibit such combination of effort. American companies have to cooperate after the fact and as a separate operation. It's very difficult to compete against the HMT type of combination this way. The flow of information becomes difficult, costly and sometimes impossible.

But give credit to the Japanese for organizing to **satisfy their customers**. After all, customer satisfaction is the heart of good business policy. The Japanese have developed some of their business practices over many more centuries than has American industry. We would do well to explore the basic business practices of those more experienced in this area of customer satisfaction.

### *The Federal Role in Transportation*
To understand how America's transportation effort works, let's look at the role of the federal government. After all, transportation is a national problem as well as a local and regional one. So the Fed's role is important.

When you examine federal transportation actions from the end of World War II to the present day, the contrast between Japan and the U.S. is startling.

At the end of World War II, Japan lost no time in launching its economic war. On our side of the Pacific, we were busy cutting duties so we could buy more consumer goods — many of them Japanese products. Everyone had to have a new car, a TV, art work, homes, electronic gadgets, cameras and all the rest.

What about our nation's transportation facilities after the war? Roads were in poor condition and getting worse. The absence of federal transportation planning during the years immediately following the war still is affecting U.S. progress years later. The public agency responsible for highways, the Bureau of Public Roads, was doing little planning, with little funding and no political clout.

By contrast, in the early 1950s Japan had plans underway for new transit systems in Tokyo and Osaka. Japan had a national policy on rebuilding commuter railroads and plans for a new high speed rail link between Tokyo and Osaka. Highway planning took second place. It was controlled!

In the U.S., the emphasis was just the opposite. Highway planning took top priority with mass transit running a very poor second. Public transit patronage peaked in 1946, then started a decline of about 6 percent a year. Highway activity began to increase at about the same rate. Automobile production was about 2.1 million, then rose about one million cars a year until reaching some 8 to 10 million.

A five-year delay in financing a highway or transit system doubled the funding required in the '50s and '60s. Many projects suffered from this dilemma.

Obviously some serious national planning had to be done, and soon. In 1954, a Committee on Urban Transportation was established to guide local communities in obtaining "the best possible transportation at the least possible cost and aid in accomplishing desirable goals in urban renewal and sound urban growth."

Noble sentiments. That statement covered the water front but did little to fund projects or provide an effective planning process. While there were many meetings and conferences, it wasn't until 1955-1956 that some meaningful things began to happen.

Under President Eisenhower in 1955, General Lucious D. Clay — still thinking in wartime terms — reported on and recommended construction of a 10-Year National Highway System to be some 37,000 miles long and funded by $23 billion in federal bonds.

In 1956, the Federal-Aid Highway Act was created. Planning for the Interstate Highway system began in earnest. But it still lacked serious federal funding or formal planning at the state level. However, progress on federal funding came with the creation of the Highway Trust Fund which raised federal taxes on fuels and broke the long-standing policy of not designating a specific purpose for federal tax income.

Then the Housing Act of 1954, which had provided funds only for small communities, was revised in 1958 to also cover cities. Many cities started planning, although mainly for highways. Transit remained a poor cousin.

President Kennedy, a supporter of federal action on transportation, had the subject investigated anew. He led the way to two landmark pieces of federal legislation: the Federal-Aid Highway Act of 1962 and the Urban Mass Transportation Act of 1964. The first of these established strict rules on urban planning. Its 10-step process is still applied today, with minor changes. The second legislation provided funding but only to be released in increments through a separate authorization process.

The Interstate and Defense Highway's program was increased to 41,000 miles and $24.8 billion, to be finished in 13 years. Although this system was just being completed in 1989, and at a cost almost double its original estimate, its benefits are many times greater than forecast.

Our interstate highway system is one of the finest federally-sponsored transportation projects of all time. Maybe a little late and very light on the maintenance provisions, but we do have the finest highway system in the world, as of now.

A warning, though. Unless maintenance improves on our highways and bridges, they will be impossible to restore. The maintenance backlog — now about $30 billion — is building up. It must be paid. The longer we wait, the higher the cost will be. Already we are talking about a new super-highway system. We'd better fix the existing one first!

### But What About Mass Transit?
Highway progress is all well and good for automobile, bus and truck travel on the open road, but what about our growing and congested cities? What about mass transit?

Much information has been flowing in countless conferences on improving transportation. But, in comparison with highway transportation, little improvement has been made in mass transit.

The first federal legislation to deal explicitly with urban mass transportation was the Housing Act of 1961. It came in response to financial problems of the commuter railroads across the country. But it provided only low interest loans!

While we were talking, Japan was acting, building two new subway lines and rebuilding many commuter rail lines. The construction of the high-speed New Tokaido "bullet train" line from Tokyo to Osaka was completed in 1963. Acclaimed worldwide, this achievement inspired many countries to improve their railroads.

HUD moved oh so slowly on mass transit. Finally, two pieces of legislation in 1964 and 1965 spun off transit from the housing agency and formed a U.S. Department of Transportation (DOT).

For public transportation of all kinds, this was an important breakthrough, long needed. Allan S. Boyd was approved as the first Secretary of the new Department. I had met Boyd when he was with The Brookings Institution. He went from there to chairmanship of the Civil Aeronautics Board. Boyd had a wealth of experience and created an efficient organization. He brought together 31 semi-autonomous agencies in a logical and workable manner to create the organization that exists today.

With the automobile and highways dominating the thinking and planning in this country, it had taken from 1945 to 1966 to bring urban mass transit into its rightful political and funding position. Actually, the Urban Mass Transit Agency, now the Federal Transit Administration (FTA), was formed officially by a legislative act in 1968. I took great satisfaction in attending the White House ceremonies and receiving fountain pens used by President Lyndon Johnson when he signed the two critical acts. And I dined twice at the White House, once with Lady Bird — a delightful woman.

### Funding Improves But Costs Go Up

Funding increases and appropriations came on a more regular basis from 1966 until the 1980's. Boston, New York, Cleveland and Chicago all received many new transit cars and assistance in financing organization improvements. Cities throughout the U.S. received many new buses, critically needed. Several major new transit systems were implemented — BART in San Francisco, WMATA in Washington, D.C., and MARTA in Atlanta. All were good systems. Late, yes, but they provided a needed minimum service on a daily basis. However, none operated automatically.

But then the cost of new transit systems started to go through the roof. There were several contributing factors. As the transit business began to show signs of important growth, the military contractors jumped on board. First came the Department of Defense contractors and then the space activities, with actual transfer of NASA people to UMTA, the public transit agency. Finally, DOT was influenced to employ the more advanced military contracting practices.

Due to the questionable progress of UMTA in attracting new passengers, Congress pulled in the reins, reduced the funds available and put limits on the funding process. It was apparent that, while the initial funding had been well spent, much lower costs and better analysis were necessary.

So the search began for lower cost solutions. The old trolley car was revived. With modifications and high tech improvements it became Light Rail Transit (LRT). Although still basically an old-fashioned trolley car system, it is now sophisticated, with improved speed, acceleration, quietness, energy efficiency, computer control and greater comfort.

LRT's are being installed all across the country, but with limited success. Costs are running over estimates and ridership is falling well below forecasts.

Rail transit systems and downtown people movers are encountering similar disappointments. For example, in Miami, a rail transit system, combined with a downtown people mover, encountered tremendous cost overruns and ridership is running 75 percent below forecasts. Detroit has a similar situation with lower patronage and greater budget problems.

In 1974, the Senate Transportation Appropriations Committee directed the Congressional Office of Technology Assessment to assess the potential for AGT systems. The OTA report the following year concluded that the $95 million spent on research and development up to that time by UMTA had not produced the direct results expected in the form of fully developed urban systems. This conclusion was reached despite the fact that several foreign countries were using our technology and considered it applicable to their cities!

*Table 1*

### High Cost, Low Ridership
### Characterize Recent U.S. Transit Projects

| Location | Length (Miles) | Year opened | Estim. cost ($Millions) | Actual cost | Forecast daily riders | Actual daily riders |
|---|---|---|---|---|---|---|
| **Light Rail Systems** | | | | | | |
| Buffalo | 6.4 | 1985 | 213 | 529 | 92,000 | 33,000 |
| Portland | 15.0 | 1986 | 143 | 214 | 42,500 | 19,000 |
| Sacramento | 18.3 | 1987 | 87 | 176 | 50,000 | 14,000 |
| San Diego | 4.5 | 1986 | | 31 | 6,900 | 4,500 |
| Santa Clara | 20.0 | 1987 | 276 | 498 | 40,000 | 11,000 |
| Pittsburgh | 10.5 | 1987 | 480* | 542** | 67,000 | 17,500 |
| **Downtown People Movers** | | | | | | |
| Detroit | 2.9 | 1987 | 119 | 210 | 71,000 | 11,000 |
| Miami | 1.9 | 1986 | 78 | 140 | 41,000 | 12,000 |
| **Rapid Rail** | | | | | | |
| Atlanta | 21.0 | 1979-86 | 1,376 | 2,500 | 578,000 | 503,000 |
| Baltimore | 14.0 | 1984-7 | 450 | 990 | 206,500 | 52,000 |
| Miami | 20.0 | 1984 | 78 | 140 | 41,000 | 12,000 |

*\* complete project estimate*
*\*\* not yet complete*
Source: *Office of Technology Assessment Report To Congress 1988*

UMTA (now FTA) was asked in 1988 to report to OTA on the last 10 mass transit projects in the U.S. (See Table 1) The data was not encouraging.

As a consequence of these disappointing results, two things are happening. Congress is further questioning transit funding, and the FTA is taking new directions in planning and funding methods. Private participation in the planning and funding is an obvious need, but the developers are hanging back.

Meanwhile, with streets and highways becoming long parking lots, traffic congestion is moving to the suburbs. A new one-year program called "Suburban Mobility Initiatives" was introduced in 1987 and was extended in 1989 for two more years. While it is important to recognize the suburban situation, it really is just a different dimension of the traffic congestion problem in the city.

These new programs are directed toward increased private participation and investment. They aim to reduce the need for large federally-supported rail transit systems and, hopefully, to develop a "demand" response instead of just tapping the commuter market. Chances of accomplishing this objective are slim, however. Just expanding the service which already lost a great number of customers will not return them to the fold.

The issue remains — patronage — how to get people to ride public transit other than simply commuting to work. The way we have been going at it, there is little demand for systems other than those which serve as a principle commuter service. And that doesn't solve the urban traffic congestion problem or the future horizontal development of our most valuable asset — the city.

# CHAPTER FOUR

# Public Transportation: the battle for funds

D id I plan my career path? Sure, twice. Then circumstances planned it for me a third time. And that's the career that stuck.

My first effort at career planning was while a senior in high school. My father had died at age 47 leaving my mother the house and $25,000. This little lady who had only a third grade education proceeded to make a comfortable living with that small nest egg by going to the stock exchange office in Newark every day and playing the market.

Well, I was good at math. If my mother with her limited education could do that well in finance, I decided I would be able to do even better with a college education. Fortunately, I never tried to make my living playing the stock market. I probably would have lost my shirt.

When it came time to select a major before my third year in college, the nation was still going through the devastating depression. A financial career didn't look so good now. But I remembered my father's advice about chemical engineering. He had worked at Standard Oil of New Jersey and had always said chemical engineers come through hard times better than most professionals.

So my career path changed. Throughout the '40s and '50s I was primarily a chemical engineer working in electrochemistry. Innovation and development of new production techniques was my field. But, in the early '60s, my attention was turned to the problems and opportunities of ground transportation.

Whether my spare-time work on off-beat technical projects — the artificial kidney was one — had anything to do with it or not, about this time Westinghouse made a decision that shifted my career abruptly. As I look back, my earlier career planning had been worthwhile even though the final shift was not my idea.

One morning in 1963 I was called into the front office in Pittsburgh and told that I was being appointed to the position of Divisions General Manager, supervising the activities of three Westinghouse operating divisions — Transportation, Industrial Repair and Welding. Later three smaller units were added — Utility Repair, X-Ray and Industrial Electronics.

Of course, each of these divisions had a General Manager who directed its day-to-day operations. My job was to provide overall supervision and coordination.

I must confess that Transportation got my attention right from the start. And it has been my area of greatest concentration ever since. Why? Because I saw there a tremendous, unsatisfied need not only in America but throughout the developed world. It represented a challenge that was exciting. It spread beyond the technical to the political and social. Engineering skill was only part of the challenge. Getting things done in the public arena was the other part. And that fired me up.

At that time, the Westinghouse Transportation Division researched, produced, marketed and serviced transit motors, controls and braking systems. And, after 1968, complete automatic guideway transit (AGT) systems and signaling were added to the line.

I struck gold at the Transportation Division right at the start. The Division Manager was a big, likable guy named Ray Marcum. Not only was Ray an excellent engineer, but he was a fine manager of people. All I had to do was get acquainted with the business and find out what I could contribute. And with Ray's guidance, that didn't take long. They didn't need much help in the technical end, but they sure felt the need for it at the commercial and political end.

The transportation business was one of those on-again-off-again affairs. One year business would be booming; the next two years nothing would happen. Customers? We had a lot of good ones. Outfits like the New York City Transit Authority (NYCTA) that ran that city's extensive subway network; the Long Island Railroad; the Penn Central Railroad; the Chicago Transit Authority; PATH, the Port Authority's Trans-Hudson service from Newark to New York City; the Massachusetts Bay Transit Authority (MBTA) in the Boston area.

Only one thing was wrong with this impressive list of important customers — none of them had any money. And most of their equipment was over-age and in need of repair.

Ray took me around to visit each of them and to become familiar with their needs, their systems and their buying habits. I soon learned that these businesses depended on getting money from the states or local municipalities. And not much was coming in. The transit authorities and the railroads couldn't keep their systems running at a level to attract ridership. The public was abandoning public transportation in droves.

### My Career Path Is Finally Set
The people in charge of these starving businesses knew very well what the problem was. On a visit to Chicago, Ray introduced me to Walter McCarter, the Transit Authority's (CTA) general manager. Walter had always been a hard man for Westinghouse to do business with — he preferred GE — but he knew his politics. When he offered to take us to lunch I got suspicious. And, sure enough, in the middle of lunch he suddenly changed the subject and put the bee on me to get involved with the Institute for Rapid Transit (IRT) and the American Transportation Association (ATA). These organizations, he said, were hard at work in Washington to get legislation passed by Congress that would provide major transit funding.

I didn't realize it then, but Walter had set the course for the next 25 years of my life — working to encourage public and private funding for transit and the development of ways to improve people mobility. That's still the pattern of my life.

All transit authorities operating bus lines, trolley lines and rapid transit systems were members of these two organizations, IRT and ATA. So were the major companies in the transit equipment industry. But there was one catch. The transit authority people held first-class status, but the business memberships were second class — no voting rights. Just send money!

Nonetheless, I got in line and went to work. I have since served on many committees of these two organizations. But the assignment that took the most time and was most rewarding was the chairmanship of the combined IRT and ATA legislative committee. That group performed the principal legislative task of both organizations during that period, 1964-68. That task, of course, was to establish an important linkage in the flow of information — the liaison with Congress.

One of the first things I learned as I met with congressmen and their staffs was how little they knew about public transportation, even in their home districts. Obviously, the first order of business was to educate these people on the problems. So we stepped up public relations efforts and launched an information program.

It seemed clear to me that we needed a professional lobbyist — someone who knew his way around Congress, who knew the key Senators and Representatives and their staffers. A lot of people don't like the idea of lobbying, but it's really a vital information function in those areas where business and politics must necessarily mix. It serves a useful public service as long as it is done with integrity. And that's the way we set out to do it.

We retained a very good man, Paul McGowan, to fill this role. And the results were satisfying. During my time as chairman of the legislative committee we followed three major bills through Congress. One provided major funding for transit, bus and rail; another funded the high-speed New York to Washington Metroliner, and the third established the Urban Mass Transportation Administration (UMTA).

Many of our strategy meetings were held in the evenings when the Senate or House were not in session. I remember one such meeting, at McGowan's home in Maryland, when the late Tip O'Neill was present. We hoped that this influential Congressman would be helpful in lining up some of the southern and western congressmen in support of pending transit legislation. We had a lot of data on their bus systems that would be useful in Tip's hands since they were not interested in rail transit projects.

The hospitality and food proved to be so good that Tip fell fast asleep on the couch after dinner. I was sitting right next to him, and, to my amazement, when he awoke a few minutes later he picked up on the conversation as if he hadn't missed a word. He assured us the bill would pass. And it did. Despite my Republican leanings, I was most impressed with his knowledge of the situation and his political acumen. But then, I was only learning what most people already knew about this man.

Other political figures weren't quite as knowledgeable. Senator Pell, who went to Japan and rode the New Tokaido bullet train at 150 miles per hour, assured everyone that the Metroliner between New York and Washington would make the same speed. No way. But, at least, he helped win the votes that passed the Metroliner legislation.

One thing our legislative committee never achieved was to gain for mass transit equal funding with highway. As mentioned earlier, the Highway Trust Fund is the only federal fund designated for a specific purpose — building highways. With the help of O'Neill of Massachusetts, Pell of Connecticut, Williams of New Jersey and other congressmen, we presented data to show that transit and railroads were just another form of highway. Nice try, but Congress didn't buy that argument.

One of the personally rewarding returns from my legislative efforts was to attend the signing by President Lyndon Johnson of the large funding bill for transit in 1966. So important was this legislation that the President had a dinner at the White House that evening for those who had contributed to its passage.

Just getting into the working part of the White House was a new experience for me. And so were the security precautions involved. You must have a written invitation and your name must appear on the approved list at the guard house where you are to enter at a specified hour.

Just before noon I appeared at the guard house. As I handed my invitation to the guard, a long limousine pulled up and I recognized inside the same Senator Pell who had ridden the high speed New Tokaido train and then started the Metroliner project. He apparently had forgotten his invitation. Despite his suggesting that his work in transportation was so well known that he should be passed through, it was no dice. He was turned back. However, he must have returned with the needed invitation because he appeared at the President's elbow when Lyndon was signing the bill.

The President must have used and passed out 20 to 30 pens. I got one of them.

The dinner was inspiring. There were about 20 people there in addition to the President and his staff. To our surprise and pleasure, Lady Bird Johnson walked in as we were talking before dinner and she invited us to take a short tour of the White House first floor with her. Our "tour guide" was most gracious and answered all questions with ease.

At dinner, I had the pleasure of sitting directly across from the First Lady which made conversation easy. Lady Bird is a smart woman — maybe smarter than her husband. It was clear from her remarks that beautification of America was her thing.

I made several efforts to get her assessment of the new mass transit legislation. It was her hope, she said, that we would be successful so that traffic congestion would be reduced sufficiently to allow more people to get into our cities. In this, she obviously shared the hope of most people for an end to traffic congestion.

Lady Bird caught me as we were leaving the table and again urged that I volunteer to help Pennsylvania in the state's beautification projects. She was a real saleswoman. Too bad she couldn't have picked mass transit as her contribution to our country.

During those early years, I received three pens from President Johnson and had dinner with him once more, again to the accompanyment of the U.S. Marine Band. You can imagine how a military band rattles the White House walls. Lyndon wasn't much for chamber music. He preferred trumpets and trombones.

### New York's "Red Book"

The problems that the transit industry had with its customers often stemmed from the fact that the transit authorities liked to hold the car manufacturers responsible for as much as possible. Take the matter of new car specifications as an example.

The New York City Transit Authority (NYCTA) had a "red book" for new car specs. They went by this book on every order for years. Before my time, I understand the book was about 1/4-inch thick. Then the government money started to flow and the red book grew thicker. During my period of responsibility for meeting customer demands, the red book doubled in thickness to about 1/2-inch, but we still were able to meet its requirements. By the early '70s it had doubled again to one-inch in thickness and trouble loomed on the horizon.

The expressed purpose of this book was to spell out in detail all transit car specifications. Public agencies tend to seek protection behind such books of regulations and specifications. These agencies play the role of the perfect expert whose position is fortified by their role as the purchaser. Communication becomes more and more a one-way street. By contrast, in other countries there is better two-way communication in transit projects. The two sides help each other. It has not always been so here.

Take this example from the early '70s when the New York City Transit Authority received funding from the state and the federal government to purchase 750 cars worth $600 million. Not only did these 750 cars have to meet all those red book specifications, but the NYCTA added a time requirement. Every single car had to work for 30 days with no more than three faults. . . all without the availability of adequate test tracks or test facilities.

What happened? Not a single car was accepted for service for almost two years. What else happened? The car builder responsible for producing these 750 cars, the Pullman Company, went out of the car business! Eventually, so did the Budd Company as well as St. Louis Car which was the first to abdicate a few years earlier.

The manufacture of transit cars has been effectively turned over to foreign competition where customers and suppliers do a better job of communicating. U.S. industry had the business and lost it, with transit authorities and suppliers both contributing to this demise. Even the defense contractors, who thought they had a new business opportunity, exited the marketplace. It's too bad they didn't persist long enough to learn how to conduct the transit business.

Japanese and Canadian companies have worked out deals to establish assembly plants with test tracks in the U.S. This makes it possible for them to meet the 50 percent U.S. manufacturing requirement for federal funding as well as supply a higher quality product owing to their sensitivity to the importance of transit quality control.

The U.S. transit business lacked the teamwork and coordination that is found abroad. In Japan, the three parties involved — transit authority, car builder and government — would get together to prepare for an anticipated business project. Information would flow back and forth among all parties.

Several years ago I walked down the manufacturing line in a Japanese factory making U S. transit cars. I could see little difference in methods used or quality achieved. It was improved coordination that resulted in overall superior performance, in my judgment. But attention to quality must be a continuing priority. Even in Japan they now are experiencing quality problems as they face the need for higher manufacturing volume in building the new high speed trains for parts of the country not served by the original bullet trains.

The transit business isn't the only place where poor communications "done us in," as Eliza Doolittle would say. You can start the list of communications disasters with the attack on Pearl Harbor where the U.S. had all the information needed to anticipate the attack before the first bomb dropped, including an operating Westinghouse radar unit that detected the first flight of attacking aircraft. Warning ignored.

Sometimes the fault is not a lack of information, but too much information or information not properly screened or analyzed. New York's red book, for example, was essentially a depository for every new or changed specification that came along. It takes more time and effort to shorten instructions and make them explicit than it does to lengthen them.

Often, the people providing information fear they are not being specific enough. But instead of being concise and specific, they get long-winded.

Incidentally, I understand the red book still exists although it's no longer red. It now requires two volumes, each about an inch thick! But, happily, I can affirm that communications have improved. The transit management in New York deserves credit for creating a better climate for the two-way flow of information with suppliers and improving the manufacture of NYCTA transit vehicles in recent years.

Sometimes the best way to communicate is through action, not words. That not only makes the information flow but drives the message home. Lou Gambicini, general manager of PATH (Port Authority Trans-Hudson) in New York taught me that. He was, of course, a customer of our Transportation Division which supplied motors, controls and other equipment for his Newark to New York subway trains that ran under the Hudson River.

One day in his Jersey City office, I was discussing the progress of a congressional funding bill when he suddenly changed the subject.

"George," he said, "did you ride the subway to get here?" "No," I replied. "I got a ride over in a friend's automobile."

"Well, on your way back to New York, do me a favor and ride the subway for at least one stop."

When I left the meeting, I made arrangements to be picked up at the next station to Jersey City which was Hoboken. After waiting several minutes on the platform for the subway train to come, I got a surprise. When it arrived, half the cars were in total darkness. I boarded one of the lighted cars. Then as the train moved through those bumpy, 100-year-old tunnels toward Hoboken, I walked into one of the dark cars. It was scary. And I quickly realized why Lou had asked me to ride the train. The fact that some of these cars were dark was **my responsibility**!

My division had just supplied new "inverters" which converted direct current into alternating current for improved lighting. Until 1964, all lights on the subway cars were powered by the same 600 volts direct current which drove the motors that moved the car along the tracks. The old lights were dim and blinked a lot with d.c. The new inverters and thyristers would fix that. But they could only handle up to 1,000 volts; larger sizes were not yet available.

Obviously, my engineers had tested our new equipment for the conventional 600 volt service and assumed that the variations in voltage — or "spikes" — on the PATH system would not exceed 1,000 volts. Surprise! When we later measured the voltage on the PATH system, some "spikes" exceeded 1,500 volts. At 1,500, the lights wouldn't work. Soon 2,000 volt thyristers became available from Siemens.

Lou Gambicini had employed the most direct method of communication to inform me of the problem. . . he made me experience it myself. Our engineers were among the best in the world. What had been their mistake? They had not tested the new equipment **under actual operating conditions** in those old tunnels before putting it into service. It was vital information they lacked — a break in the chain.

The BART people in San Francisco were to make the same "no on-line testing" mistake when they put their new system into service years later. In order to get their system in operation more quickly, they eliminated all transit car testing on the test tracks which had been provided with government funds. More about this later.

Live and. . . sometimes. . . learn.

# CHAPTER FIVE

# The Birth of Automated Guideway Transit (AGT)

A utomated rapid transit was born in Pittsburgh, but it grew up in places like Lille, France and Kobe, Japan. Why this happened is an incredible story of lost opportunity and partisan politics.

It began in the early 1960s when the community leaders of Pittsburgh realized that their famed "Renaissance" had an Achilles heel. Smoke control had cleared the air of soot and cinders. Gone were the old, broken-down buildings which had clogged the "Golden Triangle" where the Allegheny and Monongahela rivers merge to form the Ohio. A new concert hall and sports stadium were on the drawing boards. Like the legendary Phoenix bird, a sparkling new city was rising in the place of the old — except for one thing. Transportation.

Pittsburgh's public transportation consisted of an aging, inefficient trolley car and bus system and an east-west railroad system that didn't go where the city was expanding, that is, north and south. New parkways were being built to help automobile traffic but public transit was in desperate straits, financially, organizationally and operationally.

Passengers were deserting public transit and they couldn't be blamed. They couldn't count on a trolley or bus coming on schedule. And, when it finally arrived, they were crowded into a slow and uncomfortable vehicle that was too hot in summer and too cold in winter.

The Commonwealth of Pennsylvania had a paperwork transportation organization that remained aloof to local transit authorities. Nor was much assistance for city transit emanating from the Federal transportation agencies either by way of funding or planning. All in all, it was a real mess.

### The Allegheny Conference Steps In

But men like Richard K. Mellon and other "hands-on" civic leaders knew what to do about messes. They had tackled a huge one — Pittsburgh — after World War II, with the support and cooperation of the city's outstanding Mayor David L. Lawrence. They had achieved remarkable results through an organization called the Allegheny Conference on Community Development. Now they decided it was time for that group to tackle the County's transportation problem.

So it was that one day in December, 1961, the chief executives of seven of Pittsburgh's leading industrial companies received identical letters from Patrick J. Cusick Jr., executive director of the Pittsburgh Regional Planning Association which was an arm of the Allegheny Conference. With his letter, Cusick sent each corporate head a report on a recent transit study. He asked them to read it and then come up with new rapid transit ideas for Pittsburgh and Allegheny County that would meet the objectives stressed in the report.

Only one of those seven chief executives took Cusick's letter very seriously — Mark W. Cresap Jr., president of Westinghouse Electric Corporation. He sent it to his group vice president in charge of the company's industrial and control divisions, Donald C. Burnham, with instructions to "do something about this."

The assignment ended up on the desk of veteran engineer Charles Kerr, one of the company's top men responsible for transportation engineering. And Charlie Kerr enjoyed challenges. This was his meat!

I didn't know him at that moment, but two years later when I was given responsibility for all Westinghouse transportation activities, I talked with him at length about his work on this landmark project. This is his story about the origin of what we now call "automated guideway transit" or AGT.

### Kerr Finds "Room For Improvement"

Kerr started by reviewing the problems of the subway systems in New York and Chicago with which he was quite familiar. First, he told me, they cost too much to build and to operate. They were mostly down in the bowels of the city and did not present a secure environment. Their off-hour service was very poor, and even in busy periods the passengers had to wait too long for the next train. Most of their equipment was designed and built in the early 1900s and was not attractive to city officials who required new improvements in their transportation systems.

"There is," Charlie said, "a lot of room for improvement." And he set out to design an improved transit system. First he tackled the cost problem.

"Direct labor," he told me, "represents 60 to 70 percent of a transit system's operating costs, so the first thing to do was eliminate the need for an operator of the transit vehicle." In other words, automate the system just like elevator systems had been automated not too many years earlier.

"Next," he said, "the transit system of the future ought to be pulled up out of the ground for several reasons. One is cost. It costs five times as much to tunnel a transit system as to put it above ground. The other reason is to take advantage of the exciting views of the newly-built cities. Why bury transit vehicles?"

Then, Kerr decided, there must be more frequent service. Don't run long trains 5 to 10 minutes apart. Run shorter trains or single cars at close intervals, like every two minutes or less, around the clock. Since they won't need operators, this won't be expensive and will attract passengers. The rider won't feel any need to run to catch the transit vehicle if another will be along almost immediately.

Charlie added other minor improvements and started to make sketches of the system. He discussed his work with other engineers in the Transportation Division who contributed more ideas based on equipment they currently were designing and building. New solid-state electronics, for example. The engineers told Kerr they could design the propulsion and control system using new computer technology which would give exciting control capabilities and longer life with few moving parts.

They encouraged him to design a completely automated system which would stop a transit vehicle within three inches of the predetermined spot at every station and respond more safely to traffic conditions than any human operator possibly could. In other words, eliminating the operator would make the system **safer**.

Now Charlie was ready to create a final concept. He made sketches and built a small model of a transit vehicle and its guideway. It included rubber tires, two cement tracks or guideways and a center steel guide beam with horizontal wheels and tires that locked the car to the system. It couldn't go off the tracks. When all was put together, it was surprisingly simple.

### The Port Authority Plans A Demonstration
What should the next step be? The Allegheny Conference did not build things, so Don Burnham and Kerr went to the Port Authority of Allegheny County — the transit agency for the area. That agency liked the concept and decided a demonstration would be needed. Proof that the system works!

But they decided not to place an experimental project on an existing trolley line. Instead, they would build a test loop in one of the County parks. Looking back on it, this may have been a fatal error. No matter how well the experimental model worked, it still wouldn't prove safety of operation in actual public transit service. And safety was to be the main point of attack when the ensuing political battles began later on.

Nonetheless permission was granted to place a two-mile loop of the new transit system in Allegheny County's South Park and operate it for the public during the big County Fair which was held there every year.

Several variations of the new demonstration system were proposed, ranging from $1.5 million to $15 million in cost. When the specific design was agreed upon, however, the cost was $5 million. Part of that money could come from the county, the city and the state, but obviously Federal funds were needed. So a project presentation was prepared which Burnham, Kerr and the executive director of the Port Authority took to Washington. They called on the Housing and Home Financing Agency which then was responsible for public transit. Secretary Robert Coleman promptly approved more than two and three-quarter million dollars for the demonstration project.

As initiated by Westinghouse with assistance from 31 area companies, the budget for the demonstration project looked like this:

| | |
|---|---|
| U.S. Dept. of Housing and Urban Development | $2,872,000 |
| Allegheny County Port Authority | 886,000 |
| Pennsylvania Department of Commerce | 200,000 |
| Westinghouse and other contributors | 1,042,000 |
| Total | $5,000,000 |

### What Was New?

What was really new about Charlie Kerr's "new system"? Most of the individual pieces were not new. For example, rubber tires on a concrete track or guideway was an old idea. Adding a steel I beam was nothing new either. Nor were electronic components new. It was just putting all the ideas into one system that made it new and different.

In much the same way the Wright Brothers had designed the first powered airplane 60 years earlier. They had developed only one really patentable component — the curved wing. But they had combined everything else in an imaginative and well engineered way to produce the Wright Flyer. Charles Kerr used the same technique in designing the world's first automated guideway transit system. He didn't have to worry about patentable components since the use of Federal funds required everything to be made available to the public in any case.

The demonstration loop was designed and built over a three-year period. (Figs. 4A, 4B) But in the beginning, even I was somewhat skeptical of a completely automated system. Like most of the people in the Transportation Division, I had been influenced for too long by our rail rapid transit customers to whom the idea of total automation was anathema. The only one at the construction site who really was enthusiastic from the very start was our manager of operations and testing, Dixie Howell.

But as installation and testing progressed, enthusiasm grew rapidly among the whole crew. As I was walking around the site one day observing the installation of the guidebeams, it dawned on me that we really were "playing" with a $5 million model train set. I found other people also were looking at it like that.

Our enthusiasm spread to the Port Authority organization and people of the transit agencies who visited the site. Their uneasiness about automation disappeared once they sat down at the computer control console and watched the system operate. With that they came "on board."

I was spending long hours at the site. The longer I was there, the more I became aware that this project was more than a transit system. It was a new tool for safely and conveniently moving people — quiet, fast, automated. It could be an integral part of a horizontal building, performing the same functions as a vertical elevator does in a high risk structure. I coined the name "horizontal elevator" because it seemed so similar to the elevator, except operating horizontally instead of vertically.

When some people expressed doubts about the name, I ran a contest to reward whoever could come up with a new name for the new product and process. More than 500 names were submitted. Some were pretty good and some were pretty bad. "Horovator" was one suggestion. What a name for an automatic horizontal transit system! If that wouldn't discourage ridership, what would?

In the end, none of the suggested names stood up under scrutiny and the name Horizontal Elevator still stands. It is widely accepted today.

We encountered many technical problems during the three-year period of construction and test at the South Park site. All were solved one way or another but some opened us up to political sniping that later was to mount into a huge political firestorm.

One of the first problems arose the morning the system was to be demonstrated to the new Secretary of Transportation, Allan Boyd in February, 1966.

I met Allan at the County airport the previous afternoon with a helicopter. As we climbed in, he seemed a little concerned. I asked him what was the matter and he admitted he had never been in a helicopter before. Remember, he had been chairman of the Civil Aeronautics Board before taking over as Secretary of Transportation.

For a few minutes we circled over the "Skybus" site. The media had given Charlie Kerr's system that nickname for headline reasons and it stuck. I told Allan we would be back in the morning for a demonstration ride before he was scheduled to give the keynote address at the opening of the first Pittsburgh International Transportation Conference downtown.

But we blew our first PR test.

You see, the media was scheduled to get a ride on the system before Boyd got there, but we hadn't counted on a heavy frost during the night. The frost didn't bother the guideway but it froze a thin layer of ice on the electric current collectors. That wouldn't have been a problem if we would have run the vehicle every hour or so during the night. But nobody had thought of doing that.

This was the headline in that evening's *Pittsburgh Press*:

FROST ON RAILS STALLS SKYBUS.

By the time I arrived with Boyd, of course, the frost had melted and the system was working fine. That was just the first of many PR problems we were to experience in the months ahead.

Public demonstrations had been started in South Park with the County Fair of August, 1965, before the system was operated under automatic control. Then fully automated operations were demonstrated beginning in June the following year. During the County Fairs of 1966 and 1967 more than 200,000 people were carried safely around the two-mile loop. Public interest was high.

No problems, right? Wrong. Our problems were about to start. The local politicians began to choose up sides and use the Skybus as their football.

## The Political Fight Begins

Leading the attack was the minority Republican County Commissioner Dr. William Hunt, who was looking for ways to oppose anything the two Democratic majority commissioners favored. Skybus was a juicy target. Here was a new technology that would replace the beloved trolley car. Hunt used every means at his command to label Skybus as unsafe and uneconomical. Better stick to steel wheels and steel rails, he warned. And he promptly climbed into bed with Union Switch and Signal, a subsidiary of Westinghouse Airbrake Co., a local Pittsburgh firm that made conventional railway signaling equipment. The railroad and trolley car buffs joined ranks for the fray.

The battle for headlines went on literally for years. We won some, lost some. Keeping in mind the frost episode, we did score a triumph the night it snowed.

Hunt and his cohorts, who now included Pittsburgh's Mayor Pete Flaherty, had been warning of safety problems from the start: Rubber tires won't stand up. (Never mind the famed Paris Metro which had been running on rubber tires for years.) Snow and ice will stall the vehicles. Muggers will attack the unprotected passengers with no motorman there to protect them, and so on.

We looked for opportunities to blunt such arguments and found one during the First International Conference in 1966 when it began snowing one afternoon.

We quickly decided to run the Transit Expressway (our official name for Skybus) all night to prove that neither snow nor sleet would stop this vehicle from completing its appointed rounds.

From 8 p.m. to 8 a.m. as snow fell steadily, the vehicle in South Park traveled 285 miles around the two-mile loop. Snow caused no problem on the open guideway and at station stops the guideway was electrically heated as part of the system. That afternoon, the *Pittsburgh Press* headline read:

SKYBUS RUN SHOWS SNOW NO DRAWBACK.

The accompanying article quoted a Westinghouse spokesman:

"It (the test) also showed that once we sell Skybus, there will be a bus every two minutes." And he pointed out that the 12-hour run had cost only $10.80 for the electricity.

"It is almost as cheap to run a train empty at 4 a.m. as to put it in the garage,"! he added.

But Hunt did not discourage easily.

"There is no safety walkway," he complained to the press.

"How do we know if this thing will climb Pittsburgh's hills. Where is a switch? Maybe a switch can't be built for such a system." Etc.

We responded by designing an add-on project that would have a walkway, a ten percent grade and a switch. These were simple things to do but the add-on project would cost the taxpayer another $2,400,000. It was completed on budget and on time for final testing Nov. 2, 1971.

### The Switch Is Demonstrated

I scheduled a press conference and we erected a small grandstand alongside the switch location. With the exuberance of youth and inexperience, I anticipated a glorious vindication of our system in front of the media and our main antagonist.

At 9:30 a.m. sharp, I took the mike and reported that the Phase II project was completed on time, on budget and that everything worked, including the switch. In fact, I said, our switch, because of many modes of fail-safe computer circuits in the controls, would prove to be much safer than conventional rail switching and lower in total cost when all its functions are considered.

Everybody boarded the cars for a demonstration ride — except Hunt. He refused. Naively, I was not bothered by this until I read the headlines on that afternoon's edition of the *Pittsburgh Press*:

DR. HUNT REFUSES TO RIDE EXPENSIVE SWITCH.

I was learning another lesson in political tactics. Fast footwork. Seeing his safety argument in danger of disappearing, the wily Commissioner had quickly changed the subject from safety to cost.

This experimental switch had cost more than a conventional rail switch, he told the press. I had pointed out, of course, that the switch would cost less than conventional switching when all the functions it performed were included. And that later proved to be the case. But, nonetheless, the first experimental Skybus switch had indeed cost more than a standard rail switch. And the press, which always enjoyed Hunt's newsworthy antics, played up his refusal to climb aboard the "expensive system" which he still claimed was unsafe. The public must be protected!

My 20-20 hindsight shows clearly what our next move should have been. While this early testing was still going on in Pittsburgh, the French and Japanese were already putting into operation fully-automated transit systems, closely copied after our design. We had supplied to most of our important visitors drawings and detailed reports which undoubtedly saved them years of testing and much funding. At this point, we should have publicly invited Commissioner Hunt and his partner in obstruction, Pete Flaherty, to visit Lille, France and Kobe, Japan to see for themselves. We might have had to pay their travel expenses but it would have been worth it!

The story of the ultimate fate of Allegheny County's "Early Action Program" (which also included two new "buses only" right-of-ways into the city from South and East) will be told in Chapter Seven. Suffice to say here, that even though it was finally approved and funded by Federal, State and County money, the handful of opposing politicians wouldn't give up the fight. Public hearings were held. Injunctions were brought to prevent construction. In 1972, the mayors of some 15 of Allegheny County's 129 communities were persuaded by Hunt and Flaherty to join with them in bringing suit to block further progress toward a county-wide rapid transit system.

The law suit finally got to the state Supreme Court where the proponents of the Early Action Program won a Pyrrhic victory — a legal win but political defeat.

Looking back on this episode in community futility, it is apparent that Allegheny County blew a great opportunity to establish world leadership in rapid transit that would have brought thousands of jobs and a badly needed progressive image to the area.

Twenty years later, the County finally built a modernized version of the old trolley system, with motormen still at the controls. This Light Rail Vehicle system was built at a cost of some $542 million — more than twice what the Early Action Program with the new automated guideway transit would have cost. The new trolley system's ridership figures have been very disappointing, well below expectations.

Meanwhile, automated guideway rapid transit systems, patterned after Skybus — the world's first AGT system — are operating successfully and profitably in Japan and France.

Japan's first fully-automated city system was authorized in 1977 by Kobe City and went into full operation in 1981. The line runs from the Kobe central rail station to the man-made land area known as Port Island (Fig. 14C). Even earlier in Japan, a YATSU amusement park installation (Fig. 14A) first began operations in 1971. Many other Japanese systems now are operational. One of the most interesting is a real estate development project. The developer purchased a piece of remote land, added an automatic people mover (Fig. 14B) that connected with the high speed rail system and a retail center. The profits on his subsequent sale of homes in the area paid for the transit system.

France's first and very successful automated municipal transit system was built by the city of Lille during the latter part of the 1970s and went into operation in 1982. It is described in Chapter Eight.

# CHAPTER SIX

# Airports Discover AGT and Profitable Growth

W hile the struggle to sell the merits of automated transit to the politicians of Allegheny County was being carried on, a different "public" was showing interest — the planners and operators of airports across the U.S.

At that time, the big metropolitan airports for the major cities of America were encountering a major obstacle to badly needed expansion. The roadblock was their inability to move passengers on the ground rapidly and easily — from the parking areas to the aircraft. The lack of fast and convenient ground transportation systems was seriously handicapping their ability to expand airline service.

Many of these airport planners visited our demonstration loop in Pittsburgh's South Park and saw in that pioneer automated guideway system a possible solution to their problem. In the front rank of this group were the representatives from Tampa, Florida.

Tampa Airport, through the Hillsborough Aviation Authority, was facing the need to create a major new facility. The decision had been reached in 1958 to concentrate all Tampa Bay Area commercial airline flights, including St. Petersburg, at one location.

Since that time, the Authority had been going "by the book." Said one progress report: "Until May 1962, the Aviation Authority members had a relatively comfortable and safe path in front of them. The natural course of action was to accommodate the swelling volume of airport passenger traffic with a conventional air terminal, designed from a collection of components of other terminals."

This same approach had been followed for many public projects, especially for rapid transit. Just hire an appropriate consultant and leave it to him to apply the conventional methods. That was the philosophy. But Tampa was ready to change this routine, thanks to the initiative of Leigh Fisher, their airport consultant, and Authority Director Herb Godfrey. They requested the Board to abandon the normal procedure and strike off into unexplored territory.

It was here that **vision** — that essential element to progress — made the difference. Vision by Fisher and Godfrey led to a revolution in airport design.

### Eliminating The "Long Walk"

They proposed to explore how to eliminate the "long walk" — how to put the convenience and comfort of people ahead of all other airport requirements. They sought to do it by better methods, not waiting for new technology. They believed that people had been relegated to second place behind airplane logistics. In a report covering the evolution of the typical large air terminal, Leigh Fisher said there was great opportunity to employ better methods of arranging the myriad components of an air terminal.

In focusing on "better methods," Fisher was simply following the path established in the early 1900s by Frank Gilbreth for improving industrial productivity. Only now he was doing it for airport productivity.

The Authority gave Fisher the go ahead to explore a variety of possible changes in the design of the new Tampa air terminal to meet present and future needs. This was a critical but far-reaching decision that was to change all future airport design. But it was a decision not taken easily. Such radical design changes as Fisher had in mind would delay the new airport at least two years and would greatly increase political pressure on the Authority.

However, the decision also had the positive effect of focusing the Board's attention on the subsequent process. Everyone got on board with a new feeling of dedication and achievement.

Fisher and his associates studied more than 30 major U.S. airports and came up with fresh thinking on airport design. They found that the "long walks" required of passengers in 20 of the top airports were unbelievably long. At Los Angeles and New York, for example, an inter-line passenger might have to walk well over a mile. To get to the farthest gates in almost all of those airports, passengers had to walk more than 1,100 feet — that's almost the length of four football fields.

They concluded that planners up to then had designed airports to accommodate airplanes, not people. The Tampa planners were determined to put people first and limit the maximum walking distance in their new airport to less than 600 feet.

Leigh Fisher Associates were awarded a contract to design a new airport around the "people first" philosophy. In October 1963, they presented a design concept that was so innovative the Authority got worried. It was decided to proceed but with check points along the way. A design team was created with people of capability in each field involved.

### Two Terminals — Landside and Airside

The Tampa designers split their new airport into two parts — landside and airside. (See drawing) They proposed incorporating the first fully-automated airport people mover system — horizontal elevator — to provide a fast and easy link between the landside terminal and the airside satellites.

The design team held the first of its many formal work sessions at the Tampa Airport Motel October 8-9, 1963. In addition to members of the design team, a number of airline representatives and manufacturers of passenger transportation systems were invited. Our marketing manager and I were among the latter.

There were a number of people mover designs to consider: special modes of buses, mobile lounges, mini-trams, electric carts and, finally, new automated shuttle systems.

At this time, 1964, there were many companies besides Westinghouse seeking to enter this new market, most of whom have long since disappeared from the scene. The list included such firms as Walter E. Disney Enterprises, St. Louis Car, Stephens-Adamson Manufacturing, Goodyear Tire and Rubber, Montgomery Elevator, Alden Self Transit Systems, Passenger Truck Equipment and American Machine and Foundry.

Several new companies again are trying to enter the market armed with only engineering drawings and models. The principal manufacturers in the business include Von Roll, VSL, Matra, Otis Elevator Div. of United Engineering and AEG-Westinghouse.

Despite the number of would-be suppliers, the 1964 design team was apprehensive since no manufacturer yet had a system in daily operation. But we did have a two-mile test track operating daily and carrying thousands of people. So we were given the design plans and asked to visit Tampa International to review and recommend how our equipment might meet TIA's needs.

### Alternate Designs for Tampa's Landside/Airside Concept

The cover of Leigh Fisher's 1963 report proposing a design concept for the new Tampa International Airport showed two alternate schemes for the landside/airside separation.

Both involved people movers to carry passengers from the landside terminal to the airside satellites or boarding areas, eliminating the long walk. These sketches started the author on the path to Horizontal Elevator designs and concepts.

Alternate A called for one people mover to stop at every satellite — a sort of railroad to move people in the airport.

Alternate B provided individual people movers to take passengers directly to their particular satellite, saving time for each passenger and almost doubling the airport's capacity for people and planes. Alternate B was the final choice.

Thirty years later, Tampa International is still the nation's most efficient airport for moving passengers to and from their aircraft.

### Alternate Schemes - Landside/Airside Separation Concept

*Tampa International Airport*
*Hillsborough County Aviation Authority*

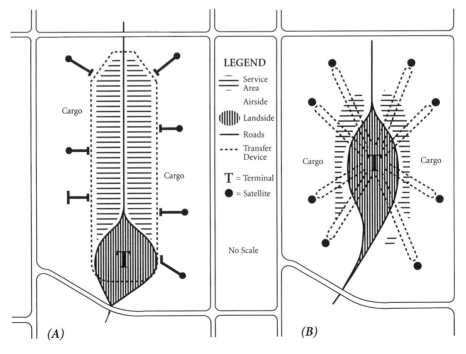

I was asked to review the problem of correctly aligning the people movers and my first suggestion was to connect all four of the satellite terminals (there now are six) with a single transit loop. Leigh questioned this, and rightly so. Most passengers, he said, would have to waste time going through satellites they were not using. And how long would passengers patiently wait to arrive at their proper gate?

To get a reading on this, Leigh had a transit car-sized plywood box built with glass windows to simulate an actual transit vehicle. Then he asked groups of passengers who were just getting off the new DC-8s if they would stand in this enclosure simulating the trip from an airside terminal to a landside terminal.

Observing their behavior, he found that passengers became restless after one minute of waiting. So he asked us to design a system that would require less than one minute to get every passenger to his or her destination — from aircraft to terminal.

This was a concept of tremendous importance for airport design and offered an important guideline for all future public transit. We now could design short increments of "horizontal elevators" to move people more frequently and for shorter trip times. This methodology would grow over the next few years into a whole new process of horizontal development and regrowth for high density areas.

Tampa's idea to separate landside and airside facilities, each containing its related services and connected by a transfer device, has revolutionized airport design. Says George J. Bean, who succeeded Herb Godfrey as the Hillsborough County Aviation Authority's Director of Aviation:

"The first-ever introduction of a passenger shuttle system into the terminal design at Tampa International Airport was the beginning of a new era in airport development throughout the world. It proved that the vexing problem of sprawling airport terminals and endless passenger walking distances could be solved in a progressive, economical manner. It proved that the needs of the airlines and their passengers could be met to everyone's satisfaction."

### Horizontal Elevators
Key to the outstanding success of Tampa International is not only the landside/airside separation concept, but the use of individual horizontal elevators from the landside terminal to each of the satellites (Figs. 5A, 5B, 5C). This gives the passengers fast and frequent shuttle service. The longest trip from terminal to aircraft-loading satellite is 52 seconds and the maximum waiting time for a passenger shuttle is 30 seconds. The passengers don't have time to get frustrated or impatient.

The design is functionally similar, of course to a vertical building with elevators that travel to the different floors. A building may have a varying number of elevators depending on the number of floors to be served. Tampa International started with eight horizontal elevators and has expanded until there are 11 at this writing.

The Tampa airport performance not only has been excellent for providing the means of smoothly loading and unloading passengers to and from airplanes, but it also has created areas which are attractive and exciting for people to visit. In addition to the ticketing and baggage handling areas, there are restaurants, gift shops, book stores, a hotel and other people services conveniently located within less than one minute of the loading and unloading aircraft, requiring very little walking. The airport terminal becomes a big shopping and entertainment mall which can occupy the occasionally long waiting times involved in air travel.

The new airport, designed with individual horizontal elevators to each satellite, opened in 1971. By 1975, when the passenger shuttles for the first four airside satellites had been in operation for three years, I knew something good was happening. People in this airport seemed more relaxed and were spending more time at the shops and restaurants.

I made a simple economic analysis at that time which showed that non-airline income was going up more than expected. In 1975 it was 40 percent and by the 1980s this non-airline income for the airport reached over 50 percent. People enjoy visiting Tampa International.

In fact, people enjoy the operation of **any** airport — when their convenience is given number one priority. Unfortunately, not all airports — even the newest ones today — have learned this, even though they may use the same modern passenger shuttle equipment.

It is interesting, for example, to compare the attitude of people in Tampa and Atlanta. The same horizontal elevator equipment is installed in both airports. However, the Atlanta airport was designed for the convenience of airplanes rather than for the convenience of people. As a result, people at Atlanta still have long walks and must go up and down escalators to a subway. So sometimes they miss their planes.

The "people first" philosophy is the key.

After Tampa International began operations in 1971 using the horizontal elevator passenger shuttle system, other airports were quick to notice what was happening. Within two years, the Seattle-Tacoma airport followed Tampa's lead and incorporated a people mover system in it's expansion plans. Miami, Atlanta and Orlando came next.

And the same type of passenger shuttle was installed at London's Gatwick Airport in 1983 — the first overseas installation. In 1989 a similar system also went into operation at Singapore's Changi Airport. The second English installation, at Standsted near London, began operation in 1990.

I find two things surprising, however. First is the refusal of most of the designers of new airports to closely copy the successful Tampa design. They seem reluctant to copy what they apparently consider to be a "competitive airport." As a result they lose much of the advantage of the new people mover technology.

### Transit Consultants Wear Blinders
Even more shocking to me has been the refusal of the planners and implementors of public transit systems generally to visit Tampa and study this remarkably successful automated transit system. They prefer to believe that what works so well for an airport, somehow cannot be applied to other public transit projects.

It's another example of the transit consultants wearing "blinders" like the ones they put on horses back in the early 1900s to protect them from being frightened by the new fangled competition called automobiles.

We still blind ourselves to new competition and hate to admit that somebody else has a better idea.

George Bean summed up the Tampa Airport experience in his annual report of 1980.

"Looking back to the mid-1960s, it was the intent of the Aviation Authority to develop a new and different airport terminal complex which would meet several basic needs. Foremost among these were:

" • Financial feasibility;
  • Increased convenience and comfort for airport patrons;
  • Creation of a showplace facility which would bring widespread attention to the Tampa Bay area, depicting it as a vital progressive community."

"Despite some initial apprehension that the new terminal complex would be too revolutionary and therefore might not be cost effective, the airport has proven to be self-supporting from its own revenues. Beyond that, the Aviation Authority has been able to maintain user charges at levels lower than those of most major airports throughout the world."

That is still the situation today.

Tampa International Airport carries out the daily operations, maintenance, planning, expansion and, most important, how it treats its customers, like a highly competitive private business entrepreneur. Public transit agencies and planners would profit by more exposure to this well-managed facility.

Recently, the public relations department has been handing out bumper stickers which read:

LUV  TIA

WORLD'S FINEST AIRPORT

People do love TIA! Why isn't that a reasonable objective for public transit in a city?

# CHAPTER SEVEN

# Pittsburgh Opts For Low Performance Transit

I promised in Chapter Five to tell you more about the battle over "Skybus" and its stormy history — the world's first automated transit system. You already are aware that the project to build this pioneering system for the City of Pittsburgh and Allegheny County was killed, probably forever. But how it was done and the lessons to be learned make an intriguing story...a drama that ends in a tragic loss for the community.

It almost takes the form of a morality play. On one side the "good guys" who favored progress, new methods, advanced technology and new industry. On the other side the "bad guys" who opposed change, fought to protect old markets, existing products and conventional technology.

If you don't like fighting and hate to see "good guys" lose, I suggest you skip on to Chapter Eight.

It is sad that during this struggle people learned to hate each other. When people love, the result is progress. But when they hate, all progress comes to a halt.

I loved Pittsburgh. Not at first, of course. When my wife and I moved to the city from the lovely shores of New Jersey, we found dirt and soot everywhere. My white shirt in the morning was a black shirt by evening. As I walked down the street I could feel cinders grate on the pavement under my shoes. It was indeed "the Smoky City."

But then we cleaned it up — a wonderful accomplishment. The "Pittsburgh Renaissance" not only got rid of the dirty smoke, it brought new highways and streets, new buildings and new businesses. Pittsburgh was on a roll into the future. It was accomplished by the whole community working together —

labor and management, politician and businessman, Republican and Democrat, a real team effort.

A lot of outsiders got into the act, too. An annual International Urban Transportation Conference was inaugurated by a group of Pittsburgh corporations. Each year the Conference attracted people from around the world to hear about new transportation systems and ride the Skybus test track. Little did we realize how many cities would adopt our ideas and copy our work.

I had visions of great numbers of people being moved by horizontal elevators in Pittsburgh and many other cities. I saw people being able to come downtown in a few minutes, never having to experience those long 10 or 15 minute waits in the rain or snow for a trolley car or a bus.

But my dream for Pittsburgh ended in a rude awakening. The drama turned out to be a modern tragedy, played out on the community stage. Here was the cast of characters:

### For Skybus

- The Allegheny Conference on Community Development and its Regional Planning Association which asked seven local corporations to come up with new transit ideas.

- Westinghouse Electric Corporation which came up with a new idea.

- The Pittsburgh Port Authority which liked the idea, demonstrated its capabilities in a test system and incorporated it in an "Early Action Program" for the County.

- Chairman of the County Commissioners Judge Leonard Staisey, Democrat, who spearheaded the transit program.

### Against Skybus

- Minority County Commissioner Dr. William Hunt, Republican.

- Mayor of Pittsburgh Pete Flaherty.

- Union Switch and Signal, subsidiary of Westinghouse Airbrake Company (WABCO), maker of conventional railroad signaling and control equipment. (Not connected with Westinghouse Electric.)

- Several small companies which had been unsuccessful bidders on the Skybus test track project.

## In The Middle

- The news media who love a good fight because it sells papers and TV advertising.

- The general public which didn't know who to believe but had the most to gain or lose.

## The Background

Pittsburgh's efforts to build a better transit system started way back in 1906. Since that time, scores of studies were made and reports issued. In the early years of that period, the public was reasonably satisfied, particularly after the improved PCC (President's Committee) trolley cars were installed. The President's Committee was a joint effort by leading corporations in 1931 to design a better trolley car, which they did.

But after World War II, things went downhill fast. The privately-owned Pittsburgh Railways system was in a rapid decline. Customer satisfaction was sacrificed in a desperate and futile search for profits.

The end result was the formation of the Port Authority of Allegheny County (PAT), which has maintained a well qualified organization over the years. PAT bought out the Pittsburgh Railways and took over all bus, trolley and river transit operations in 1964.

PAT, however, was in the difficult position of serving two masters, one public and one private. Representing the private sector was the Allegheny Conference on Community Development, a creation of Richard King Mellon and other Pittsburgh business leaders. On the other side was the political leadership of the city and county.

But PAT's Board was determined to move ahead. It shared the vision of people moving with greater mobility and enjoyment. I've already described PAT's search for new transit ideas, its construction of the demonstration loop for the automated AGT system which the media dubbed "Skybus" and its successful efforts to find funding for an "Early Action Program." By 1970, it looked for all the world like Pittsburgh would be the center of a new transportation industry and would be the site of the world's most advanced transit system providing new benefits for the citizens of Allegheny County.

Then suddenly a threat appeared. Opposition to the transit program was taking shape. It had substance and gradually form and organization. In my innocence, it never had dawned on me that anyone could fail to share the vision of a wonderful new transit system that also would result in a new industry for Pittsburgh. But some people not only failed to share it, they bitterly opposed it.

### Partners In Opposition

In the forefront of this organized opposition were two natural partners: a private company seeking to protect threatened business interests and a politician seeking to win votes by opposing the establishment. The company was Westinghouse Airbrake (WABCO), created a generation earlier by the same Pittsburgh industrialist and inventor who later formed Westinghouse Electric — George Westinghouse.

WABCO's business was the manufacture and sale of conventional railroad signal and control equipment. Why was WABCO upset at the prospect of the Skybus system? Because that new automated system was controlled and operated by computers that would make unnecessary the type of control products marketed worldwide by WABCO.

Skybus computers used very small solid state diodes and chips which required much less energy, only 16 volts and no moving parts in the braking and operating control systems. One of WABCO's profitable products was a 64-volt mechanical railroad relay used the world over for railroad control systems. It was by far the best product of its type on the market anywhere.

WABCO saw the handwriting on the wall for its mechanical relay if the low voltage, no moving parts computer system came into popular use.

I became aware of the impact of the new computer systems on WABCO and we made a proposal to that firm to join with us on the new business of automating existing trolley cars. But it was no dice. The ill-feeling grew between the two companies and we now had a bitter opponent to automated transit.

The politician with his love for the traditional railroad was a natural ally for WABCO. He was Dr. William Hunt, the minority County Commissioner. In Allegheny County, the Commission is made up of three individuals — two from the majority party and one from the minority. That meant that Allegheny County, where Democrats held the majority, had a commission of two Democrats and one Republican.

So Bill Hunt, the Republican, was looking for ways to win political points and ultimately votes by opposing his opponents on the Commission who were in the forefront of the Early Action rapid transit program. Chairman Leonard Staisey, in fact, was perhaps the chief spokesman for the proposed automated transit system.

Legally blind, Leonard was one of the most remarkable public servants I have ever known. His physical limitation certainly didn't slow him down as far as I could determine. And his mind was razor sharp.

Using time-honored political tactics, Dr. Hunt spoke out against Skybus at every opportunity. Despite an absence of technical support, he opposed Skybus as "unsafe, too expensive, untried" etc. Another factor was Hunt's hometown. He was a resident of McKeesport, a blue collar town just up the Monongahela from Pittsburgh. McKeesport commuters benefited from an unprofitable railroad train that carried them to and from the Steel City morning and evening. Steel-wheel on steel-rail was their thing. Not only that, but the proposed Skybus line would be built not to McKeesport but out into Pittsburgh's South Hills, predominantly a white collar area.

So WABCO and Commissioner Hunt joined forces and fought the battle against Skybus together.

### Flaherty Joins The Alliance
Then Pittsburgh's Mayor Pete Flaherty joined the alliance. He was the exact opposite of former Mayor David L. Lawrence who had cooperated with and even inspired the business establishment in the famed "Pittsburgh Renaissance." Flaherty generally opposed anything the Pittsburgh business establishment wanted.

The Democratic mayor found the alliance with the Republican commissioner a marriage of convenience. The odd couple had a common foe — Skybus which they both wanted to kill, and the Port Authority which had no room for an inefficient commuter railroad.

The fight was bitter. Delaying legal actions were part of the opposition strategy, with safety and cost the main points of attack. Almost daily personal attacks were launched against the individual proponents of the Early Action program. Several times I was threatened at public meetings with statements like "the death of people killed by your system will haunt you forever."

As for the safety issue, UMTA, the Urban Mass Transit Agency, had an independent appraisal made of the validity of the proposed automated transit system. It found and reported that the system was safe and indicated its full support of the program.

During the public battle, Dr. Hunt lost his seat on the County Commission in the election but this did not slow him down. With remarkable political agility he was able to get himself appointed to the PAT Board of Directors, arguing that he was better informed on transit than other candidates for the position. Nothing was farther from the truth.

But as an opponent of automated transit, he was superb. In danger of losing the battle for public opinion, he turned to the courts. He convinced 15 mayors of County communities to join with him in an equity suit to block construction of the Skybus system and stop all expenditures on the Early Action Program. A 69-day hearing was held in the County Courthouse in 1972 and on July 24th, an injunction was issued.

The trial on the Hunt and Mayors equity suit was presided over by Judge Anne X. Alpern who made no secret of her enthusiasm for rail transit. She frequently complimented the president of the defunct Pittsburgh Railways which PAT had to rescue. And she ruled in favor of the opposition.

On appeal to the State Supreme Court, however, the decision of the lower court was overturned by a 6 to 1 margin. We had won the legal battle, but Hunt kept the opposition organized and the political fight continued.

The ex-commissioner pounded away at what he called the unproven, unsafe and costly operation of the Skybus system. We presented data to refute the allegations, but the press gave more ink to the opposition which yelled the loudest and fought the longest. They were fighting, they claimed, "to protect the people."

While we at the division level of Westinghouse were free to make our positive data available, and we did, we were inexperienced in political in-fighting. Hunt and Flaherty were masters at it.

At the top, Westinghouse Corporate management made a policy decision to stay above the conflict and say nothing. Let PAT do the talking, was the strategy. I've always believed this was a serious mistake. At one point during the critical period, a press conference actually was planned for a Westinghouse top management spokesman, but it was cancelled. The claims of the opposition went largely unanswered by corporate top executives. And it was an outstanding Westinghouse engineering development that was being killed here.

Our "stay above the conflict" policy was not the way to win a battle for public opinion. When your position on a public issue is being distorted and twisted out of shape, you must get into the fray to make your position clear and the correct facts known.

While we were keeping our powder dry, our international competition (France and Japan), armed with our reports and experience, was proceeding with the construction of fully automated systems, saving much valuable time and development money. Those systems today are in successful operation.

In the end, the Pittsburgh battle ended in compromise, which was tantamount to defeat for automated transit. Unfortunately compromise has been a common strategy for political leadership on public transit issues across the country. Compromise usually means giving up the new and innovative and settling for the conventional.

In this case, the compromise called for proceeding with an exclusive "busway" — a separate right-of-way for buses built on the existing Pennsylvania Railroad line — to the eastern suburbs. And it led to eventual approval for a Light Rail Vehicle line to the south — a modernized version of the old trolley car. But automated transit was killed, thus yielding to France and Japan leadership in this field, based on the Pittsburgh designs. Pittsburgh could have been No. 1 in the world with fully automated municipal transportation 10 years before it was done in Lille, France. Instead the city opted for low performance transit and surrendered industry leadership to overseas competitors.

The Pittsburgh transit system now requires a subsidy of millions of dollars every year. Its 1992 deficit was about $10 million.

### Some Lessons
There are lessons to be learned from this community fiasco.

First, transit efforts must not be permitted to be negatively impacted by compromise and the conventional advice of transit consultants. Such people do not have any organized research and development capability. Leadership and vision is not their forte. Their civil engineering is fine. They build good bridges and tunnels. But their capability to lead us in innovating people-sensitive transit improvement is poor.

Second, the proponents of the new system, the advocates of change from the conventional, were timid when they should have been bold. Inexperienced in political warfare, they permitted the opposition to employ scare tactics and constant distortion of facts to sway public opinion. They should have employed someone experienced in rough and tumble political battling to lead an organized campaign that would sell the County's Early Action Program on its merits. The product was excellent. It just wasn't "sold."

I was to learn later that the benefits of automation in transit — lower cost, more frequent service, greater safety — were not enough to get people involved. To get maximum benefit from new methods, horizontal transit had to be built into horizontal construction and development, just as vertical transit is integrated into high rise construction and development.

Fortunately for society, automated transit survived this initial defeat. AGT systems around the world are carrying well over one million passengers a day, with an outstanding safety record. Unfortunately, the U.S. has the initiative only in the airport applications. The larger city systems have been built by foreign firms.

In 1988, Westinghouse sold majority interest in its Transportation Division to AEG, a subsidiary of Daimler Benz of Germany. Now known as AEG Transportation Systems, the firm produced by early 1993 more than 160 automated people movers for nine U.S. airports with several more under study (Fig. 6A). AEG also is opening the international market with five systems installed — three in England, one in Singapore's Changi Airport and another at Frankfort Airport in Germany (Fig. 6B).

The business is growing not only for airports but for cities. The company also has produced components of mass transit systems for New York, Toronto, Honolulu and Philadelphia. AEG employs more than 1,100 people and continues to expand.

My love for Pittsburgh was battered by the local Skybus episode, but not my love for the cause for which we fought. My enthusiasm for the opportunities we have to move people in our cities with greater ease, convenience and safety is stronger than ever. Everything required for our cities to grow without traffic congestion is at hand. All we need is the vision and intelligence to use it. Simply stated, we urgently need to improve our planning to include integration of the factors affecting horizontal growth — highways, people transit, living and community development.

# PHOTOS

*Fig. 1A. If we designed vertical transportation for buildings like we design horizontal transit, a downtown building might look like this exaggerated sketch.*

*Fig. 1B. Private architects changed our vertical mobility. This hotel has six businesses in vertical alignment. More people go up; so do profits.*

Fig. 2A. Walt Disney asked for a sketch (above) showing how transit could come into the lobby of his Contemporary Hotel. Fig. 2B (below). How it looked after construction.

Fig. 2C. An aerial view of the Contemporary Hotel at Walt Disney World shows how the monorail train runs right through the building.

Fig. 2D. Walt Disney visited the Westinghouse Skybus site in Pittsburgh in 1966, seeking people mover ideas for Walt Disney World. He adjusts his tie in the window of a test car while the author looks on.

# Early Trolley Cars

*Fig. 3A. 1897 Parlor Car*

*Fig. 3B. Golden Chariot 1906*

*Fig. 3C. Open Car 1900*

*Fig. 3D. English Double
Decker 1924*

*Photos courtesy Seashore Trolley Museum, Kennebunkport, Main.*

Fig. 4A. First fully automated public transit system, two-mile loop, South Park, Allegheny County, PA, 1965.

Fig. 4B. Demonstration system carried passengers each year from 1964 to 1968.

Fig. 5A. Tampa International, first automated airport shuttle system. There were eight people movers in 1971, now 10.

*Fig. 5B. A 1982 view of Tampa International. Ten years later, a 2,000 vehicle parking garage was built above the parking area shown here.*

*Fig. 5C. Artist sketch shows 1994 Tampa International with expanded parking facilities and an additional people mover. This doubled the airport capacity with <u>no increase</u> in walking.*

Las Vegas Airport

Orlando

Miami Metromover

Pittsburgh

Las Colinas

Orlando Terminal

*Fig. 6A. U.S. airport people mover market expands to nine installations. Las Collinas is commercial complex.*

Fig. 6B. AEG increases its
international installations to
five, with more planned.

*Fig. 7A. Lille, France Metro, fully automated transit service every 50 to 72 seconds or sooner.*

*Fig. 7B. Glass "elevator doors" at all Lille stations.*

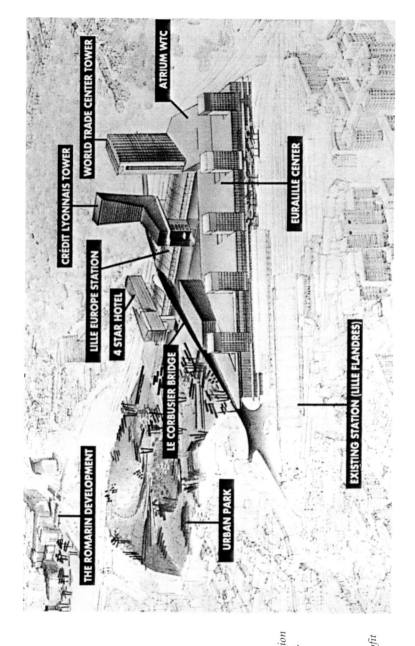

CRÉDIT LYONNAIS TOWER

WORLD TRADE CENTER TOWER

ATRIUM WTC

LILLE EUROPE STATION

4 STAR HOTEL

EURALILLE CENTER

THE ROMARIN DEVELOPMENT

LE CORBUSIER BRIDGE

URBAN PARK

EXISTING STATION (LILLE FLANDRES)

*Fig. 7C. EUROLILLE —
Here is what transportation
improvement is all about.
This Center in Lille
integrates automated
transit, high speed rail,
tramways, buses, and
auto parking. Result is
development, growth, profit
and services for people.*

*Fig. 8A. New car for Bay Area Rapid Transit District, San Francisco.*

*Fig. 8B. Washington's Metro system crosses Potomac bridge to avoid traffic congestion.*

*Fig. 8C. Metropolitan Atlanta
Rapid Transit speeds past bumper-
to-bumper highway traffic.*

*Fig. 8D. Miami, Florida Metro.
Metro-Dade Transit Agency.*

*Fig. 9A. Early Otis air-supported system connecting two hospital buildings with horizontal elevator.*

*Fig. 9B. Another Otis privately-built, air-supported system connects downtown Tampa, FL with developments on remote Harbour Island. Notice the very isolated station.*

*Fig. 9C. Circus Circus
horizontal elevator in Las
Vegas. See how the track
pedestals disappear into the
building construction, to
provide walkway.*

*Fig. 9D. Westinghouse people mover on the circulating system in downtown Miami is difficult to access.*

*Fig. 10A. A main street in Munich, Germany before it was limited to pedestrian traffic.*

*Fig. 10B. Now many people activities take place on areas once clogged with auto traffic. Here crowd gathers in front of famous City Hall Glockenspeil.*

*Fig. 10C. Intercept parking garages in Munich get people out of their cars at edge of walking area.*

*Fig. 10D. Elimination of traffic makes former street areas marketable.*

*Fig. 10E, 10F. Walking streets make
alleys attractive, bringing more
people and more business downtown.
Kiosks help sell goods on the streets
for shops 3 blocks away.*

*Fig. 11A. When Gothenburg, Sweden covered this street, retail sales went up and a downtown retail mall was created.*

*Fig. 11B. When this walking street was roofed over using steel beam supports, an office building was built on top.*

*Fig. 11C. After this street in Gothenburg was roofed, they realized that the store fronts could be removed creating an exciting new type downtown mall!*

*Fig. 11D. Covering streets meant shopping more hours a day. This photo was taken at 9 p.m. Lots of night-time shoppers.*

*Fig. 12A. An AEG Maglev vehicle (for low speed application in Germany.*

*Fig. 12B. A Japanese experimental high speed Maglev vehicle. Both Japan and Germany report experimental Maglev systems capable of 300 mph.*

*Fig. 13A. First generation Japanese
Shinkansen "bullet train" (late 1950s),
carried passengers at 150 mph.*

*Fig. 13B. Bullet trains now exceed
180 mph and some have double-
decker cars.*

Fig. 13C. First generation French TGV ("Trés Grande Vitesse") train. Second generation TGVs reach 186 mph. Through the window, utility poles disappear and the passing scenes are beautiful.

Fig. 13D. Newest Horizontal Elevator cars in Charles de Gaulle International Airport (Paris, France) to reduce walking.

*Fig. 14A. Japan's first fully automated transit vehicle (1972) runs on 400 meter loop at Yatsu Amusement Park. It also runs as a complete system (1982) for a private developer (Yamaman Real Estatement, Co.) outside Tokyo, Japan.*

*Fig. 14B. Portliner, Japan's first fully automated **city** system, provides service from Kobe to man-made island city (1982).*

Fig. 14C. Otis downtown people
mover runs from Tampa to
Harbour Island developments.

Fig. 14D. AEG automated transit
system on the island of Oahu, Hawaii
carries passengers from parking lot
into the Pearl Ridge Mall.

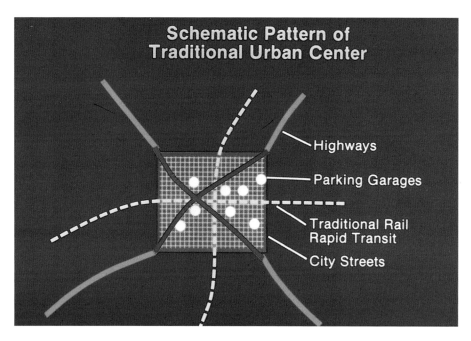

*Fig. 15A. Traditional urban center pattern leads to gridlock.*

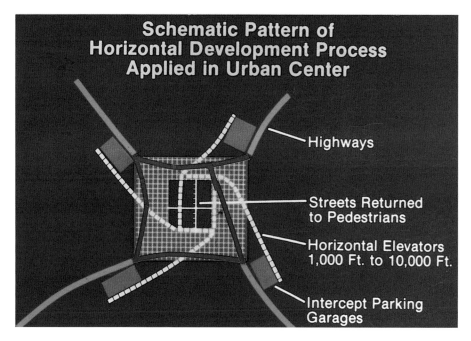

*Fig. 15B. This automobile intercept pattern permits additional growth without traffic problems.*

Fig. 16A. Horizontal elevators in architect's
drawing integrated into buildings take people
where they want to go, not just to stations.

Fig. 16B. This large urban center was designed
to integrate three developments, served by
horizontal elevators (architect's drawing).

# CHAPTER EIGHT

# In Lille A Mayor Made The Difference

While Pittsburgh was turning its back on automated guideway transit, the French city of Lille was doing just the opposite, thanks to a progressive mayor who made modern rapid transit his personal goal.

For some years before 1960, this city of about one million people in the northeast corner of France had been studying how to upgrade its public transportation system — much like Pittsburgh had been doing. The region was growing and there was pressure on the mayor to develop the suburbs, particularly to the east. A study carried out in 1969-70 had examined the feasibility of transportation improvements for the newly created Lille-Est district.

While this study was under way, Lille representatives made two visits to the Westinghouse Skybus demonstration site in Allegheny County's North Park. They expressed great interest in the idea of a fully-automated transit system and returned to France armed with reports and records of our experience.

Following their transit study and visits to Pittsburgh and other cities, the Lille officials created a Metro organization on April 24, 1970. In 1971, a major decision was as made by the Metro to develop a **fully-automated** transit system.

Important to the eventual success of the city's automated transit project was the personal interest and enthusiasm of M. Arthur Notebart, Lille's Urban Community President and the Deputy Mayor of Lomme. I know that the French transit agency COMELI and the MATRA company had most to do with the technical development of the VAL system, but the mayor was the political catalyst who put it over the top.

Unlike Pittsburgh's mayor who publicly condemned the automated system as unsafe, Mayor Notebart put all of his energy behind an automated Metro line for Lille-Est and urged full development of the area. During the years that followed, he made many presentations on the new transit system. He attended every event involving new equipment and new station openings. He informed the people of Lille that the Metro cars would come along in half the time of a conventional system, cutting waiting time in half. He pointed out that the system would be quiet because it would ride on rubber tires, not steel wheels. He stressed the creation of thousands of jobs, many of which would be permanent since a new industry was being created. And he predicted that transit equipment would become a new export business for the area.

I visited Lille many times from 1973 until my last trip in September, 1993. What a contrast with the Pittsburgh experience where the mayor joined with a county commissioner in opposing such a transit system for Allegheny County.

Exploring the first application of a totally automatic public transit system for a major city required touching many bases. I recall discussing our project in its early stages with Dr. Lillian Gilbreth, the eminent expert on productivity and workplace efficiency. She warned me that we would need four things for the project to be successful: physical feasibility, public acceptance, financing and political support. We had three of the four. But lack of that fourth — political support —doomed the project.

In Lille, however, Mayor Notebart made sure that political support was solid. Thanks to his efforts and those of the Metro organization, the French Ministry of Transportation announced on September 28, 1973 that it had evaluated the automation proposed for Lille and accepted the principle of full automation for a public transit system. This was an important step forward since it implied acceptance by the powerful public transit agencies of Paris.

### The Public Is Invited
Public exposure to the project began with the announcement of the contract award to the French firm MATRA for development of the first two experimental automated vehicles. When these vehicles were operated on a test track, the public was invited to witness the testing. The public was kept informed from the word "go" and confidence was built through effective communications.

In 1981, two years before the system was to go into operation, the first four stations were completed. Even at this early date visits were planned and promoted by the Mayor and his staff. Visitors came not only from Lille but from countries around the world. Lille gained international exposure of its "VAL" system. VAL stands for Vehicle Automated of Lille.

Before the VAL system went operational another interesting piece of news was announced. The urban community formed a joint venture with MATRA, the manufacturer and supplier of the VAL system, to manage the operation of the Metro for five years. This was to ensure the highest quality of operation and maintenance of the new fully automated process for the safety and satisfaction of the public.

The management contract with MATRA was a brilliant stroke, particularly because of the preventive and protective maintenance provisions under which a supplier would be directly responsible for the safety and reliability of the equipment and system. Both the planning organization and the transit agency no doubt were influenced by the provisions of the Tampa International Airport contract with Westinghouse. It provides that Westinghouse would have to pay a heavy fine for every "down-time" over 10 minutes on any of the shuttle systems. In 20 years, however, no fines have been assessed because no such down-times have occurred.

In Pittsburgh, the Port Authority had suggested to the mayor and county commissioners that the automated guideway transit system be tried out on the first four stations of the existing trolley line which was to be replaced. The idea was vehemently rejected as too dangerous. I was denounced for proposing a plan that would "kill people." Our experimental loop had to be located in a county park.

How different it was in Lille. When the first vehicles and first four stations of the Lille system were ready for operation, a public affairs campaign began. From April 3 until July 27, 1982 this portion of the new system was opened to the public and more than 200,000 visitors took the five-minute ride in each direction. Each Tuesday afternoon, students from various local schools were invited to ride. More than 50,000 students were thus educated on the new system. Other groups such as pensioners joined the parade of people exposed to the first fully automated city transit system before it was closed on July 27 to complete the system construction.

The French public was not only enthusiastic about automated transit but was eager for it to begin full service. (Figs. 7A, 7B, 7C). What a contrast to the negative position of the Pittsburgh officials who feared to expose the people to such innovation.

### Form VAL Network
Mayor Notebart's enthusiastic support of the Lille Metro continued actively for two decades, 1968-1988. The new Mayor, Pierre Mauroy, has continued this

support and has placed new emphasis on growth for other French communities through modern rapid transit. Bordeaux, Strasbourg and Toulouse joined with Lille to form a VAL network. The objectives were twofold: a common analysis of problems such as financing, material orders and work progress, and also improved dialogue with ministerial authorities and builders.

Elected officials, administrators and technical service managers of these four major urban centers of France thus meet regularly. It seems to me that cities of America would profit from this type of enlightened cooperation on their common problems and services.

Unlike America, the French recognize the value of standardization. For example, of their some 80 nuclear power plants, most are of one design — the Westinghouse pressurized water reactor which they licensed years ago. This is not the case in the U.S. where practically every nuclear plant is custom-built to the specification of the owner utility company. Now standard design is being pushed for French transit, too, using the VAL system.

What happened in Lille when line number one went fully operational? Patronage went up sharply. This represents one of the first times in post World War II history that a transit system developed a "demand response" instead of just a commuter response (see graph). In Lille, the public transit patronage was 47 percent higher than before the Metro was installed and patronage is still rising. Obviously, the Metro is pulling people out of their automobiles. This caused great joy in the city and led to construction of a second line (Line No. 1 Bis). Further extension of the system is already under way. It reaches a new station on the TGV (high speed rail) line which connects London and Paris via the tunnel under the English Channel.

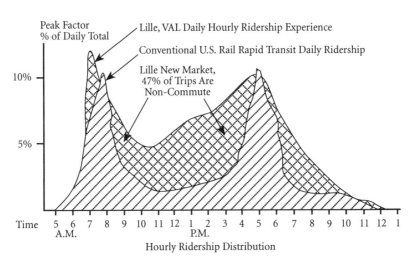

Hourly Ridership Distribution

Patronage of Lille's automated line #1 has grown at a remarkable rate — 21.1 million in 1984 to 29.4 million in 1988. After the second line came into service in 1989, the patronage reached 48 million by 1992 and continues to grow. Obviously new markets have been reached.

The outstanding achievement has been to attract riders **outside** the conventional rush-hour peaks experienced by rail rapid transit systems. This new ridership represented **new** business for public transit. Forty-seven percent of the trips in Lille are not commuter-related since, obviously, there were not 47 percent more jobs created in the area.

This new market was achieved by providing higher performance in meeting the needs of people. The factors in this higher performance include: service every minute; the honor system of fare collection; better alignment of the system in the downtown area with free circulation; the high quality of maintenance, and the non-transit type stations which are architecturally designed with emphasis on beauty.

Such fine ridership led SCNF, France's national railroad, to make Lille the only stop on the newest high speed TGV Atlantique line (Fig. 13D) running between Paris and the "chunnel" to England.

This added station on the Metro system also by 1994 will connect Line 2 of the Lille Metro with two nearby urban centers — Tourcoing and Roubaix. By 1995, Lille should have the finest transportation system in the world.

What about financing? Lille explored every possibility. The City Council discussed the matter with private businesses and the business community responded. Every employer with over nine employees agreed to an assessment of 1/2 percent of wages at the time of start-up and an increase every year until the amount reached a maximum of 1 1/2 percent. This encouraged the federal government to provide additional funding.

With the patronage running well above the level forecast, both regional and federal assistance were readily available.

The Lille experience has had great influence throughout France and the rest of the world. In November, 1987 the Association of Paris Transport chose the VAL system to connect the Antony Station of the Paris RER with Orly International Airport. Service on the new 4.7 mile Orlyval line began in October 1991. It runs at four-minute intervals during the morning and late afternoon busy hours and seven-minute intervals the rest of the day.

No city has the mobility convenience of Paris and its Orly International Airport. Orlyval connects the airport to the regional transit system RER which is connected to the Paris Metro and Charles de Gaulle Airport. There is some question, however, as to how to keep this link operating because of high trip costs. With it, an airline passenger can reach any part of Paris without stepping outside.

VAL systems are now being built not only in the French cities of Bordeaux, Toulouse and Rennes but also in Jacksonville, Florida, at Chicago's O'Hare Airport and in Taipei and Barcelona.

When the decision was made by Lille officials in 1971 to proceed with the first fully-automated transit system the financial risk was great. It was taken by people with vision. An International Transportation Conference held at Lille in September, 1993, celebrated 10 years of safe and exciting operation of the automated VAL Metro system. The author made a presentation at this conference based on the subject matter of this book.

Lille has good reason to be celebrating. Its transit system has achieved the highest performance in public transit history and is attracting such added benefits as being awarded the only station stop in northern France on the high speed TGV-Atlantique railroad system. The transit success was a key ingredient in Lille's choice as the site for the new Eurorail Center. Known as Euralille (photo 7C), the site will be an interchange for high speed TGV trains, automated transit, tramways, buses and a 6,000 car intercept and parking facility.

# CHAPTER NINE

# Rail Rapid Transit:
# A Tale of Three Cities

R apid transit began with construction of the first London Underground line in 1853. Originally operated by steam, The Underground was converted to electricity in 1891. The first U.S. subway was opened in Boston in 1898 and New York followed in 1904 .

Ground level rapid transit — a much less costly undertaking — evolved after the turn of the century when electrical pioneers like George Westinghouse saw the possibility of harnessing the new alternating current to electrify horse-drawn trolley lines.

Indeed, one of the early rapid transit lines, the Dayton, Springfield & Urbana Interurban Railway, caused the Wright brothers a problem as they attempted to conduct test flights of their early airplanes in relative secrecy on the outskirts of Dayton, Ohio in 1904. This trolley line between Dayton and Springfield ran alongside the farmland where Wilbur and Orville were experimenting with the Wright Flyer. In fact, the first five-minute airplane flight in history was witnessed by two officials of the Interurban line who were passing by on an unscheduled run and stopped to watch.

Such trolley systems became known as "rapid" transit simply because the trolleys ran on steel rails over their own right-of-way, permitting speeds greater than was possible by the early automobiles or horse-drawn vehicles on the unpaved roads. And they didn't have to stop at every street corner.

An early application of rail rapid transit was made in another Ohio city, Cleveland, in the 1920s. Also built on its own right-of-way, "The Rapid" ran (and still runs today) between the suburb of Shaker Heights and the center of downtown Cleveland. This line was simply a trolley car system but one which was free of traffic delays and made a limited number of stops.

From construction of the Shaker Heights Rapid to the mid-century, rail rapid transit changed hardly at all. The few lines built still were simply regular trolley cars running on their own right-of-ways. A motorman up front did the driving and collected the fares.

Then came automated control and modern transit cars.

Suddenly, all a city had to do to solve its traffic congestion problem, or so it seemed, was to install a rail rapid transit system. Federal legislation, which we all had worked so hard to obtain, now provided that the government would pick up 80 percent of the billion dollar cost. It would create new jobs and spark private development.

I confess that I used these words in speeches across the country from 1964 until the 1970s to market transit cars and automated signaling systems. Most companies involved in the transit business, including my division at Westinghouse, were profitable for the first time in many years. We believed that the golden age for mass transit had arrived!

We were wrong, but this fact didn't become clear right away. We were encouraged by the fact that major rapid transit projects were launched in three big cities — San Francisco, Washington and Atlanta. (Figs. 8A, 8B, 8C).

### San Francisco's Automated BART System
The first formal steps to get started on a new transit system were taken by San Francisco business and political leaders in 1949. They were concerned by the growing traffic congestion in the region and the detrimental effects it was having on the local economy. In 1951 the state legislature established a Bay Area Rapid Transit Commission and the engineering firm of Parsons, Brinckerhof, Hall and McDonald was retained to conduct a transit study. The study began in 1953. After three years, the firm recommended that a heavy rail system be built to extend throughout the nine county Bay Area.

In response, the state legislature created a Bay Area Rapid Transit District (BART) with very high hopes. The new BART system "was to be automated, fast, comfortable and attractive." So says the BART IMPACT study which was written in 1979.

The BART District made a good start. For one thing, it developed its own source of funds, local bonding. Once they had a billion dollars to spend, BART officials moved rapidly, issuing requests for proposals (RFP) in 1966 for design, construction, vehicles and signaling.

My division responded directly to the signaling RFP and indirectly through the Rohr Aircraft Manufacturing Company of San Diego for all the electrics and braking on the transit vehicle.

I must admit that I was somewhat concerned about the signaling proposal. We had developed a whole new computer-controlled signaling system for the two-mile-long Automated Guideway System in Pittsburgh's South Park. This computer control had operated three vehicles over a four-year period quite successfully. But a 75-mile big city system with more than 400 vehicles in daily service was a large step up.

I spent many hours in the downtown Pittsburgh offices of my boss Chuck Hammond, who was the Industrial Group Vice President. He grilled me on our plans, designs and pricing. Both of us recognized that we could either make a good profit or lose our shirts on this pioneering project. This was high risk business, and even more so for us because transportation was still struggling to establish itself as a solid component in the Westinghouse mix. It had never made much money in the past. Maybe this would be a breakthrough.

Was automated control of a big city transit system feasible? We were convinced that it was. So was BART. But nobody yet realized the troubles we were to run into before the system would run smoothly. I guess it is a good thing we didn't.

We bid approximately $52 million for the transit car order with the Rohr Company — about $25 million for Rohr and $27 million for Westinghouse. And we bid approximately $24 million for the complete computer-controlled signaling package. At 1993 prices, each of these orders would be triple, or higher, what they cost BART in the 1960s.

Without the South Park two-mile demonstration project near Pittsburgh, it never would have been possible to bid these projects. At South Park, we already had transported more than 200,000 people safely with only a computer driving the system, night and day, in all kinds of weather and with changes in schedules.

We felt confident about our bids because they included money for installation of the new signaling system on a test track that BART intended to construct. Unfortunately BART had suddenly dropped its plans for the test track. BART's General Manager Bill Stokes told me this was done to avoid being accused of helping the various bidders. It turned out to be a bad mistake.

The good news was that we won both orders. But our troubles began as soon as the first Rohr transit cars were ready for testing. It was quickly apparent that

Rohr did not have enough experience in the rail transit industry to produce a satisfactory product on the first try.

We had developed an automated electrical testing machine which we used daily at our West Mifflin, Pa., plant to make some 40 tests on transit vehicle electrical systems. Rohr could not get a single one of its first transit cars to pass these tests.

I had just returned from Japan after investigating manufacturing facilities and transit products there. Even before getting over the jet lag, I headed for San Diego to examine Rohr's new cars. And when I looked at the underside of the first car, I couldn't believe my eyes. Instead of the neat, uniform lacing and combed wiring harnesses I had seen in Japan, the Rohr wiring looked like spaghetti wound over, under and around all the electric motors and braking components. What a mess!

The cars had to be entirely rewired, systematically and with a combed look in the final design. The job finally was accomplished and the cars passed the tests. But our troubles were only beginning.

### Gophers In A Goldfish Bowl
We were living in a goldfish bowl. The entire rail transit world was watching the construction and progress at BART. Headlines appeared on the front pages of newspapers in Europe and Japan whenever problems surfaced.

One day a car broke through the sand pile at the end of a spur and hung precariously over the road. A lovely picture of this embarrassment appeared on the front pages in Pittsburgh, San Francisco, London and Tokyo.

Even gophers got into the act! And they almost shut down the entire 71-mile-long system. Here's what happened.

The entire BART system is divided into one to two-mile blocks of signal control. When a train is on one block, no other vehicles are allowed to enter that block until it is shown to be empty. This is a standard safety requirement around the world in rail systems.

Suddenly, we began to get signals indicating that a car was in a block when actually there was no car there. And this became more frequent. If it continued, we were out of business.

At South Park we had never encountered such a problem and we wracked our brains to investigate everything possible that might be giving a false signal. It took us several months to solve the mystery.

Finally we located the culprit — gophers. And in the Bay Area, they have lots of gophers. These animals loved the taste of a new material we had used to cover the cable tubing. It was made of Teflon Polytetraflourethylene, a very hard and strong material that was difficult even to cut into with a sharp knife.

But gophers have very sharp teeth. Inspection of the cables from above had revealed nothing, but we found the gophers were biting into them from underneath, sometimes causing a short in the copper wires. The short resulted in a signal to the computer that made it think a car was present on the track. Of course it wasn't a car, it was a gopher having his lunch.

We had to lift, inspect and replace an awful lot of cable and then lay it in a bed of Gunite which is a cement-like material that hardens and covers the cable entirely. It was the end of free lunch for gophers, but the press had a field day at BART's and Westinghouse's expense.

### Test Period Is Ignored

Such problems wouldn't have been so bad if the original plan for the test track and for a six-month testing period prior to public operation had been followed. But in their hurry to get the public on board, BART officials ditched this sensible plan in favor of letting the public use the system long before that test period was finished. What a terrible mistake!

In September 1972, the first BART line went operational. Interviews with the riding public showed that people were pleased with the quality of the ride, and I knew from experience that it was better performance than anything in Europe or Japan. But the problems that should have been confined to test runs now began happening with an impatient public on board and with the ever vigilant press watching.

One of the biggest problems was maintenance.

I always had believed in preventive maintenance, and Westinghouse had just completed a maintenance agreement with the Hillsborough Aviation Authority at the Tampa Airport designed to **prevent** problems. There we guaranteed "on time" operation of the vehicles, with Westinghouse committed to pay thousands of dollars for every 10 minutes of "down time." To assure on time operation, Westinghouse contracted to handle all the maintenance. The Aviation Authority actually operated the eight people movers (now 10) **without having any employees** on the system. The only employees were our maintenance people. And the arrangement worked beautifully.

When we tried to negotiate a maintenance agreement with BART management, however, the Board wouldn't buy it. We proposed to train their new employees over a six-month period on how to maintain the vehicles and operate the maintenance shop. It would have required about six Westinghouse employees in San Francisco and the whole deal would have cost BART about $1 million. But no deal.

As a result, within a year cars that were out of service began to line up outside the shops. Much of the trouble was due to motor problems. We guaranteed BART 2,500 hours "mean time before failure" on properly maintained motors, and we kept a supply of motors nearby to cover Westinghouse warranty failures. But we proposed that BART order new motors at once to replace those failed due to inadequate maintenance and beyond warranty. It required three months for motors to be manufactured and delivered after an order was received.

BART, however, ordered no new motors as motors failed. As many as 200 cars were down at one time. Of course this made front page news in San Francisco and Pittsburgh.

Meanwhile, down in Sao Paulo, Brazil, a new and very similar transit system was operating, and the Brazilians had accepted the Westinghouse proposals on operation and maintenance. Their system never had more than five cars out of service at any one time. And I understand that, occasionally, they even operate a train with no operator or attendant on board — quite similar to the Westinghouse airport people mover installations.

Despite its early headaches, the BART system now runs well and has proved to be a major advance in public transportation. Automated control has proved itself. The BART train of cars has an attendant sitting up front, but he doesn't drive the train. He is there simply to press a button that will safely stop the train should he determine that an unsafe condition exists. I expect this system will perform even better when the BART management recognizes the broader responsibility involved in operating a major rail transit system. Here's an example of what I mean by that.

One very rainy day in San Francisco I was at the Walnut Creek Station on the BART line and noticed that the parking lot next to the station was half empty. This was surprising because I had just come from a meeting at which the BART Board was wrestling with the need to expand the parking lots. Walnut Creek, they had said, needed more parking space most of all.

I phoned Bill Stokes, BART general manager, and asked him to meet me at the Walnut Creek Station and I would buy him lunch. When he arrived, I asked him to look at the Station and the half empty parking lot. Where were the people?

I had just been studying designs of transit system stations around the world. In Paris, one of the large downtown stations was renting the areas around the boarding zones for displays of outdoor furniture from the department stores above. It was a good example of service to the transit passengers. Why, I suggested, doesn't BART do something to make its transit stations desirable places to visit and shop. Maybe then rain wouldn't keep people from riding the transit line.

Well, Bill Stokes saw the point. He promptly established a station redevelopment committee to go to work on the problem. But guess what happened. A couple of weeks later Stokes was asked to resign. Wouldn't you know!

I knew I was on to something important, however, and I continued to probe. That led to what I call the Horizontal Development Process which is described a little later in this book. It is clear that the day of the isolated transit station is gone. The transit lines of tomorrow must run into the places the public wants to see, visit or shop. The "station" must help make a profit and provide a service to the transit customer. It cannot be just a place to get on or off a train.

### Washington Builds Its Metro

Perhaps the greatest need for mass transit in any American city at this time existed in the nation's capital. Traffic to and from Virginia and Maryland was bumper to bumper every morning and evening, five days a week. It's even worse today than it was in 1960. Just imagine what it would be if the Washington Metro hadn't been built!

Lured by the promise of billions available from the Federal Government for mass transit systems, the Washington Metropolitan Area Transit Authority (WMATA) was formed in 1966. It took over all the private, failing and decaying bus companies and purchased hundreds of new buses. Believe me, they were appreciated by the residents of our nation's capital.

Then the planning started for a major new rail rapid transit system. Everyone knew it would be terribly costly, but weren't they close to the government coffers? Costs zoomed to almost $4 billion for all the new buses and the rail transit system. One thing must be said, however. Ridership on this system is still going up while most urban transit systems are having trouble maintaining passenger levels.

WMATA had good fortune right at the start. They found a top notch man to carry out the Metro construction. Many of us in the ATA and IRT organizations were on a search committee. I'm not sure who first located General Jackson Graham, a retired officer from the Army Corps of Engineers, but they found a good one.

General Graham did an excellent job in a politically difficult environment. And I say this despite the fact that my company lost the signaling contract. We did win the contract to supply the vehicle propulsion system as well as the escalators which used a new standardized unit design. Manufactured in standard sections, the escalator units only required joining at each end, with no structure underneath. At the Wheaton Station the 230-foot escalator was the longest in the world in the 1970s.

I had several meetings with Jack Graham on station planning and development. With the enlightenment gained at BART, I was particularly interested in getting the Metro station located within or immediately adjacent to the National Airport terminal. And I presented several ideas for doing this.

Jack finally told me to forget it. As you know, there now is a long walk, with baggage in hand, from the Metro station at the airport to the terminal buildings — across streets and in rain and snow if the weather is bad.

Jack explained that he had had several meetings with the officials of Alexandria and Fairfax County. Locating the Metro station in the airport vicinity at all was difficult enough without trying to get it inside the terminal buildings.

"My job," he said, "is to get the system built on schedule and as close to budget as possible. I'll miss both targets if I attempt to combine the Metro and the terminal facilities." Furthermore, he said, he wanted to retire soon and spend some time with his grandchildren.

It is interesting to note that now, two decades later, the Washington Metro and the airlines have started a project to combine the transit station with a new airport terminal building built out over the street, exactly as we had recommended. Too bad it couldn't have been done that way originally. WMATA is nonetheless a fine rapid transit system of 75 miles and 64 stations. It continues to grow, from 34,438,000 passengers in 1979 to 140,400,000 in 1993 total transit system. No other U.S. rail transit system is showing increases year after year.

Several of WMATA's stations are surrounded by what I will call speculative joint development, even though they are not actually integrated. That's not ideal but it's better than nothing. We are learning, slowly.

### Atlanta Follows Suit

The third major American city to opt for a new rail rapid transit system in the 1960's was Atlanta — hub of the South.

The Metropolitan Atlanta Rapid Transit Authority (MARTA) was created in 1965 and became the engine of continuous and aggressive effort by the Atlanta business community and the city to do something about their growing traffic problems.

In the fall of 1971, the city got the approval of the voters for a one percent sales tax to be dedicated to transportation. This approval was limited by the fact that two less-populated counties — Clayton and Gwinnett — withdrew, while Fulton and DeKalb moved forward. MARTA became an operating agency when it purchased the privately-owned Atlanta Transit System, also in 1971. Atlanta was on its way!

MARTA continues to make progress with additions in some of the areas that first were passed over. One reaches the busy Atlanta International Airport in the south and another Doraville in the north.

I have vivid memories of my visits to Atlanta at the invitation of the Central Atlanta Progress organization to evangelize the potential of building a people mover — horizontal elevator system — for the downtown area. Westinghouse already had installed the people mover at the airport.

They told me I had to convince the Mayor. I tried. During my several meetings with Mayor Maynard Jackson he seemed most interested and I thought I had him convinced, but nothing happened. Looking back on it, I kick myself for not yet having had enough experience to realize the need to include private developers in those discussions.

However, we did make an impression on the MARTA team, and they created some of the better stations, partially integrated with bus and rail interchanges.

MARTA has been reasonably successful and a good investment for the community. Additions are being continuously planned, even with reduced Federal funding. This progress must be particularly appreciated because Atlantans really love their automobiles. They have provided a major network of excellent highways in and around the downtown area and lots of parking garages. There are excellent hotels and motels in and out of town. So it is a real test ground for public transportation.

I hope the extension of the transit system to the airport will be better patronized than are most other city transit connections with airports. Combining the transit system with exciting interfaces and eliminating the long walk into the airport would provide great incentive for its use. We'll watch how well this is done, or not done, in Atlanta.

### A Fourth City Add-on Is Not So Successful — Miami

This "Tale of Three Cities" would be better if it stopped with three. But we must add a fourth — Miami — because federal funding became available.

By the early 1980s there was serious doubt in Congress about the wisdom of funding any more large rail rapid transit systems. But Florida's Dade County felt strongly about the need for transit help. Miami was growing more rapidly than most other cities and downtown congestion was becoming horrendous.

A tremendous job of funding was done to make possible construction of a 20-mile full-scale rail rapid transit system with 20 stations, plus a Downtown People Mover (DPM) with 10 stations over a two-mile stretch.

I am familiar with the DPM funding procedure since I had proposed funding by private business interests in the city on a **sole source** basis. They enacted a business tax in Miami, the amount depending on how close the business is to the DPM.

When the DPM was bid, all quotes were over $120 million and were declared unacceptable. To solve this problem, a new price was structured by Westinghouse that would leave out some of the engineering and duplicate insurance coverages and would guarantee that Westinghouse would not have to pick up the cost of unexpected city problems. This made possible a negotiated, sole source price of about $108 million. The entire system, including real estate, came to $170 million.

Reports currently indicate, however, that total cost of the DPM equipment has now risen over $108 million.

I had a chance in 1990 to inspect how well the people mover system had been integrated into development when I attended an International People Mover Conference in Miami. Some of the supervisors told me I would especially like the transit station located opposite the new Hyatt Regency Hotel. It was built into the building right across the street, they said.

As I registered at that hotel I could look across and see the automated cars stopping at that station. When I asked the hotel clerk to direct me to the station, he had to carefully write down the instructions. It required a circuitous walk down escalators, through tunnels, across the street and into the basement of the building. Then two escalators took me up to a platform **outside** the building. It was impossible to get into the building without going back down the escalators, into the basement, then up an elevator to the reception area. I timed it. It took me 12 minutes to take a five-minute ride. No wonder patronage of the Miami DPM is less than one-third the volume forecast. And the main Metro Dade rail system has had even less response.

The Miami downtown people mover has two major shortcomings. There is very little integration with commercial development and its circular routing fails to achieve the valuable traffic intercept mission. The equipment operates reliably enough but ridership has fallen to a fraction of that forecast. They added two intercept links to the north and south which further increases the already high capital cost. No private developer ever could afford such investment.

What have we learned from these big city transit projects of recent years?

First, it has been proven that fully-automated control of a big city transit system is feasible. It works, it's safe and it's economical.

Second, with escalating construction costs, subways will be so costly that future projects must almost certainly be above ground and integrated into buildings. Washington probably was the last major subway project.

Third, to be successful any transit system must take people quickly and easily where they want to go — not force them to take a five minute walk in the rain to get where they want to go. People will ride when offered real convenience and comfort. Planning that provides auto interception to cut out congestion and integrates transit with development is the key.

Is there another approach to bringing mobility back to our congested suburbs and center cities? What about the private developer?

Otis and VSL have several private projects operating at low cost. Since the early 1970s an Otis air-supported (no wheels) people mover system has been in service at Duke University Hospitals (Fig. 9A) connecting hospital services and parking.

Similar Otis equipment connects downtown Tampa, Florida with new developments on Harbor Island (Fig. 9B).

Several successful private examples of people movers are found in Reno and Las Vegas at Circus-Circus Enterprise hotels. They integrate a number of businesses, parking, hotel rooms, gift shops, restaurants, circuses and the gambling casino. (Fig. 9C).

If private developers, with their technical capability and business acumen, are to become involved, there must be the conventional expectation of profitability in the projects. There is considerable profit in private development, especially when land values are included. But we must recognize that we have not delivered a quality performance in our cities. In vertical development — tall buildings — the methods are well known and the profits are there. But horizontally, much improvement is required.

# CHAPTER TEN

# Needed: A Change of Direction

The spring of 1975 awakened me to the urgent need for a change of direction in public transportation. Maybe it was the result of seeing the transit projects in San Francisco, Washington and Atlanta fail to deliver up to projections. Or maybe it was just the distillation of everything I had experienced since first entering the transit field many years before.

But it suddenly became clear to me that public transit issues and projects were pawns of the political bureaucracy. Every politician seemed to have one pet "single function" solution to cure all public transit ills. It was virtually impossible to discuss with any politician the real effects of public transit projects on **people** — the potential transit rider — and on **development**.

Each official I contacted in government or in planning circles seemed to possess a pre-conceived conviction about what was wrong with public transit. This conviction usually stemmed from one earlier experience or one discussion with someone in the transportation field or one article recently read. I found a plethora of "instant experts."

For example, in 1967 one U.S. senator took a ride on the new Japanese high speed "bullet train" at 150 mph, then came home and introduced legislation to put 150 mph trains on the Metroliner run between Washington and New York. Did our poor roadbeds make any difference? Not to him.

My division at Westinghouse won half the contract. But we soon found that it was not possible to run trains over 85 mph on most of the track between New York and the nation's capital. Over one short stretch near Princeton the train could reach 120 mph for a few minutes, occasionally ripping off a pantagraph in the process. Both Westinghouse and GE, the other supplier, lost money on the project and we still are nowhere near running trains at 150 mph in the U.S.

Amtrak has tested on the Metroliner run a Swedish train that uses a stabilizing principle first demonstrated by Dr. Clinton R. Hanna, associate director of research for Westinghouse. It tilts the cars as they round curves to counter centrifical force. It is said to make possible speeds up to 150 mph on the existing track. These trains will be available sometime after 1996.

Dr. Hanna's principle was first developed to stabilize the guns on American and British tanks during World War II and was given much credit for enabling British forces to defeat Rommel in the decisive battle of El Alamein which turned the tide of Nazi advance in North Africa.

After the war, when we applied the stabilizer principle to trains on the Pennsylvania Railroad in the early 1960s, it was done only a single car at a time, not for an entire train as the Swedes are doing it now.

Both Japan and France now are operating trains at more than 180 mph while we lag well behind. In addition, Germany has developed and is operating ICE (intercity express) trains at speeds over 160 mph. These high speeds are achieved not only by using technically good equipment but also by building and daily maintaining exactly straight and very level track.

During the early Metroliner project, we simply hadn't done our homework. Decisions made at the top were not based on information gleaned from the public at all. They usually were based on meetings of political officials and "transit experts." And these "experts" most often were the same people whose transit planning had been delivering declining performance for decades.

### "Take It, It's Good For You."
Transit authorities in government were deciding what was good for people and prescribing it like medicine. "Mr. Taxpayer, this new subway will be good for you, so use it!"

The three multibillion dollar transit projects then underway in the three major cities impacted differently on different constituencies. For the labor unions, the projects meant many new construction jobs. And how they supported the lobbying! For the city fathers they meant a lot of new money poured into the local economy. For real estate speculators they meant land values would go up in the vicinity of a transit stop or station.

The politics of lobbying for transit was complex. Everyone ground his own political ax. I saw very little promotional or educational effort aimed at developing a city or an area with planning based on changes the modified transit system would bring. Earlier, I had taken a helicopter ride in Toronto to observe how its subway system had affected growth and land use in the area. Even there I was disappointed. Growth did not follow the transit system.

What did the people think of these three major projects? They assumed that traffic congestion would be ended. Not because **they** would ride public transit, but because they believed **other** people would.

I worked hard for more than three years in Washington to help get key legislation passed. We were successful in getting some three billion dollars a year for public transit. But doubts overwhelmed me. Were we doing the right thing? Would this great investment of funds and the tremendous intrusion of massive structures for miles into the center of three great cities actually solve the problems as we claimed?

Scenes from my visits to the Walnut Creek Station of BART in 1974 kept flashing before my eyes: the rainy day, half-empty station parking lots with heavy automobile traffic continuing to rumble into San Francisco over the two long bridges. What was happening here?

My compatriots in the transit industry didn't share my concerns. They kept their heads down and concentrated on maintaining the flow of government funding for transit at the federal, state and local levels. Even the people in my own company seemed to be interested simply in selling equipment for new transit systems, not in figuring out how to make public transit work.

### Who's Working On Solutions?
Somehow, nobody appeared to be worrying about what it would take to get people out of their automobiles to use the new systems. They would get out because they should. That was the accepted philosophy. I assumed that a solution that met people's needs would be exciting; that people would be happy with the improvements. That was in the 1960s and '70s, and it is little different in the 1990s.

When I worried about the situation with my corporate hat on, it became a matter of markets. Were we realistically developing a growing market for our new products? We were experiencing some large cost overruns in transit projects at that time. And our hometown of Pittsburgh had cast a large shadow over automated transit by rejecting it in favor of conventional trolley car technology.

It should have been apparent to the planners that municipal growth patterns were changing. People were moving to the suburbs in large numbers. The shopping malls and new outlying business complexes were revolutionizing commercial life. They were drawing people out of the city centers, leaving only commuters to travel "downtown." The joy of shopping downtown in our cities was dying.

Joel Garreau would say that this was the beginning of Edge Cities, those edge-of-town centers which have the characteristic of being business-only cities with the automobile the principal method of transit.

Pittsburgh's 5th Avenue was a small copy of New York's 5th Avenue in the 1950s–1970s. But by the 1990s many stores were boarded up, specialty shops had departed for the suburbs and downtown 5th Avenue in Pittsburgh was a "no man's land" by 9 p.m. — this despite a new high-rise with an exciting atrium lobby at the foot of the street. Obviously high-rise buildings alone do not bring people downtown or keep them there.

Things were different in Europe where exciting patterns of shops, hotels, parks and pedestrian streets were arising in the center of cities like Munich, Gothenburg and Stockholm.

At the same time, new transit ideas were coming on stream from many sources. Automated guideway transit of the type we had developed was just one of these, of course. In an exhibition of new automated transit developments (Transpo–1972) at Dulles Airport just a year before, there had been introduced a similar system wherein the vehicles, riding on air, were pulled by cable, not individually propelled by their own motors. This meant lower costs, with just one motor propelling a number of cars and a much simpler signaling system.

Although this system was limited to from 5,000 to 10,000 feet for each increment, Otis had just received an order from the Duke University Hospitals to link several hospital buildings, a warehouse and parking.

It was apparent that technology was moving on a number of fronts, but in what direction? I was finding that the transit authorities, the federal agencies and local planners were simply not interested in looking at **new methods** because people weren't responding. They just wanted to look "down the track" and raise more funds to build conventional systems. Ideas on horizontal development improvements were too fraught with problems. They might slow down a project, cost more, stir up new legal questions, etc.

### Wanted: Innovation In Methodology
I was convinced that what we needed now wasn't necessarily more new technology, but new directions — innovation, but in methodology rather than just technology.

In search of better answers, I began to visit private developers and architects to pick their brains. One was Bob Fairburn. As previously mentioned, Bob was a past president of AIA and president of his own development company. I told him about my new Horizontal Development Process and he showed quick interest.

"George," he said, "what you ought to do is create a cookbook on your process."

I was puzzled. Why in the world would I make a "cookbook" on such an important subject as national rail rapid transit. But Bob went on to explain what he meant by cook book.

"What is needed is a logical process in simple steps that the average citizen can follow," he continued. "Something like a recipe in a cookbook which can be studied and reviewed by others."

I gave this conversation a lot of thought and pondered a career decision. To pursue the type of investigation that was needed, I would have to break my 39-year-long tie with Westinghouse and launch my own effort. Some five years earlier I had set up a proposed consulting firm anticipating that someday I would make a full-time project of my transportation experience. Now, I concluded, the time had come.

I talked it over with many friends both inside and outside the company. My immediate superior, Dr. S.W. Herwald, vice-president engineering, said he thought that the Transportation Division, an operating unit, was losing interest in the broad application of transit systems. They spend more time on the hardware, he said.

"Find a position in the research division," he suggested.

Well, I was in the age group to take early retirement if I so desired. So I retired from Westinghouse and set up my own transit consulting business. I was determined to pursue the idea that what public transit needed was a new direction — innovation in methodology and approach to the problem of public mobility. Public transit had to be integrated with commercial development and with the activities of **people**.

This work, I felt, would not only be interesting but result in a new mobility and happiness for people in our cities. What better goal could I set for the rest of my career?

Innovation and methods improvement was nothing new to me. After all, I had spent from 1956 to 1962 in manufacturing development, seeking new and better methods of making products. In 1956, Don Burnham had come to Westinghouse from the Oldsmobile Division of General Motors where he had acquired a reputation for manufacturing improvement and better methods. Naturally, he was my kind of guy.

I had worked with Don for several years earlier, applying my Westinghouse electroplating developments on Oldsmobile bumpers. He must have approved of my work because, shortly after he joined Westinghouse, I was appointed manager of the newly established Manufacturing Laboratory at the company's R&D Center.

Now that was behind me, but I had learned a lot about methods improvement. It was to stand me in good stead. Today I am a methods enthusiast in the transportation field. And, believe me, it's really needed.

There is far too little effort being made on the introduction of **new methods to achieve greater public mobility**. The secret lies not in the **invention of new ways to transport people**. It lies in imaginatively integrating and combining the inventions of the past two decades. There is plenty of good technology. We must learn how to make it work to give the public real mobility.

We have to get across the idea that "innovation" doesn't refer only to technology. It also means new practices and procedures in moving people. It means applying new transit technology with methods that take advantage of the new characteristics of the technology. For example, complete automation permits transit vehicles to come along one car at a time every 55 to 72 seconds as in the Lille, France system. There is no need to have 8 to 12 vehicles in a train to reduce the cost of an operator. Hopefully, when the public understands this single fact they will insist on frequent service — quite similar to the frequency they get in a high-rise building's vertical elevator system.

### The Dead Hand Of Politics
Unfortunately, politics puts a deadening restraint on such changes in methods and procedures. For example, this is an area where new methods and new business relationships can bring private developers, their architects and their investment into the upgrading of public mobility. But politicians resist yielding authority to private entrepreneurs over what they consider "government projects."

The new methods of integrating development and transit should drive projects, not transit technology or the transit agency. In the Edge City, business developments and the automobile control the growth process and transit is mistakenly considered a high density solution not presently needed.

Encouraging the private developer to design, construct and operate horizontal transit to serve his development is seldom done. Transit is not considered to be his business. But, of course, it really is. He creates the exciting malls and business complexes. His expertise is urgently needed to bring excitement to mobility in our cities.

In the spring of 1988, I was invited to participate in the Transportation System Center Colloquium series at Cambridge, MA., on "The Needs and Opportunities for Transportation in the 21st Century." Each speaker repeated the clichés about higher performance possible in the future, and then alluded to the need for increased Federal funding to accomplish it.

The Federal Highway Administration speaker passed out a questionnaire which asked for our (favorable) opinion on the need for a new, larger center under federal auspices so that work now done at the state level could be better handled by the federal government. He said our "votes" would help this cause along.

I didn't fill out the forms. More federal control is not the answer.

Recently, the administration's 1991 transportation policy was established by D.O.T. Two key policies represent a major change in direction for funding public transit. Most far-reaching was the shifting of half the $151 billion trust fund down to the states for application. And the decision to use the money for either highways or transit was left to the states, within limits.

The second policy change was to increase private participation in public transit — something long needed. These two new policies should stimulate the introduction of innovative and more efficient public transit — an exciting trend if the transit is integrated with people activities.

After that 1988 meeting my exposure and interest broadened and I got involved in the program first started in 1982 called SBIR, Small Business Innovative Research. Its first objective was "to stimulate technological innovation."

After several meetings in Washington and Boston, I responded to a suggested project to investigate and recommend new methods of "privatization." I won a SBIR contract and investigated public-private applications of automated guideway transit in France, Germany, Japan and the United States. Some of these AGT systems were patterned after my own work with Westinghouse in the late 1960s.

My work, completed in six months, was submitted in a report complete with color photo prints. Only those who successfully complete a Phase I project are permitted to submit a Phase II project.

A Phase II project is for the implementation of a plan to construct a system or increment of a system to the designs reported on in Phase I. I submitted four possible projects with letters from four cities recommending their partnership increments.

What happened? Nothing. I doubt if the Phase II report ever was seriously studied by either UMTA or TSC. When I inquired about it some time later, I was told no funding was available for future Phase I or Phase II SBIR projects.

### Transit Needs a "Change of Heart"
The heart of transit planning up to now has been reliance on government funding and centralized direction from Washington. Clearly that has failed. A group of transit officials and consultants sitting around a table in Washington to decide what the public ought to want isn't the answer.

Hopefully, the 1991 shift of half the funds to the state level and encouragement of more private participation indicates a realization of this fact.

Certainly transit needs a change of heart, transplanting the old "let Uncle Sam decide" with a new heart that says let **us** decide. "Us" means the local entrepreneurs, developers and their architects who need to bring people into their hotels, shopping malls, sports arenas, amusement parks, airports, apartment complexes, high rise office towers and other centers of activity.

These private businesses have the will and the resources to get the job done. And they know what it will take. No, private developers cannot take over the whole public transit mission, but certainly they can and should provide key increments of our urban transit networks, and do so at a reasonable profit.

Walt Disney understood as do some other successful entrepreneurs that transit must not only be efficient, it must be **fun**. People will ride something that gives them enjoyment — that's what driving an automobile does. When I was discussing with Disney the idea of bringing his monorail directly into the lobby of his Contemporary Hotel at Walt Disney World, I suggested bringing it through at the second floor level. That would be best for security, I believed. But Walt said "No, let's bring it in at the fifth floor level, that will be more exciting for the passengers." And he added, "never mind the cost of raising the level of the concrete pedestals, that's negligible."

Today's transit planners must take that cue. Transit that is interesting and exciting will attract riders. The people who say "getting there is half the fun" have the right idea. It's the private developers who understand that philosophy, not government officials and conventional transit consultants.

The heart of public transit from here on must be private initiative, not government, and it must be exciting technology that gives people a good ride for their money. No two systems must be alike or limited to one kind of track. Private developers will explore all kinds of systems and designs. People always respond to a good product and good service.

# CHAPTER ELEVEN

# Growth Planned From Within, Horizontally

For the last half century, a lot of city growth has been vertical. Look at the skyline of almost any major city and compare it with photographs of that city's skyline at the end of World War II. Much higher buildings occupy the downtown areas today.

These high-rise buildings have been developed over the last few decades as separate facilities — each like an oasis in the city. New vertical transportation technology — faster and quieter automatic elevators with computer-controls to minimize passenger delays, more and better escalators — has permitted taller buildings with improved efficiency of people movement.

But what about the ground level transit that people must use to get from one building complex to another? Such horizontal systems have been constructed only as "add-ons" to the vertical growth. With just a few exceptions our ground level transit is simply upgraded circa 1930 technology: buses and trolleys, even rail rapid transit, with a driver up front collecting the fare as you enter or leave. And this ground level transit growth, **where people are**, plays second fiddle to streets and expressways.

This lopsided process which encourages vertical growth efficiency but discourages similar attention to efficient horizontal growth has been "protected" by a transportation bureaucracy of federal, state, regional, county, city and local transit managers and consultants. This long line of transit managers usually starts with the Secretary of Transportation in Washington and extends through the many governmental levels down to the manager of the local transit authority at the city level.

I know a great many of these people. They are experienced transportation managers and specialists, generally competent and intelligent, who start out with the best of intentions. So why has their performance been so lackluster at best? I believe it's because political demands and pressures gradually overwhelm them. They are forced to limit their thinking in order to keep "on the track."

Take the case of Allan Boyd. As I have already pointed out, he did an outstanding job of organizing the U.S. Department of Transportation. Since then, he has held several top level positions in the railroad industry.

Last year, Mr. Boyd was invited by the National Academy of Engineering to address a Conference on Engineering and Human Welfare. I couldn't believe the talk he delivered was by the same man I had known. It was filled with generalizations and innocuous comments. Allan came out strongly "against sin," so to speak, and for increased Federal capital investment. He was for innovation, competition and all those other good things. It was typical of what I call "cubbyhole bureaucracy." Allan obviously has fallen victim to political pressures and demands.

He mentioned the desirability of closing streets to force vehicles to the perimeter and displace congestion to other areas. That's typical government thinking. The way it was done in Munich, Gothenburg and other European cities was to attract more people downtown but intercept more automobiles and thus reduce traffic congestion in the center city. Later in this chapter I will discuss this process further. It is possible to increase people activity at lower capital cost.

Alvin Toffler in his book "Power Shift" talked of cubbyholes and channels which are features of modern bureaucracy. And his description of bureaucracy fits the transportation field to a "T."

We group the facets of transportation technology into various cubbyholes and then each cubbyhole channels its ideas throughout the bureaucracy. Every idea or element is kept in its own cubby-hole and circulated in its own channel. The latest is LRT — Light Rail Transit. It is cubbyholed into its own channels not unlike those of the trolley car.

### Private Developer Isolated
For example, the private developer is kept isolated from the design, construction and operation of transit systems. The developer always is invited to pay fees but never design a new transit system that is intended to serve his commercial development. He is kept in the developer cubbyhole. He isn't supposed to get into the transit cubbyhole where the transit consultants operate.

Thank goodness for Leigh Fisher, an unusual airport consultant from San Francisco. He broke out of the transit cubbyhole and got into the developer cubbyhole. With just a little help from our team, his designs and ideas enabled Tampa International to achieve the best commercial performance of any airport in the world, according to several competitive ratings. Tampa International Airport gets more than 50 percent of its income from non-airline businesses. It now has six corridors with horizontal elevators moving people every minute day and night with trip times of no more than 55 seconds. No one has to walk more than 600 feet to get to or from his flight.

An 8,000 car intercept parking garage is now being added with the 11th people mover to continue the "no long walk" policy.

In my hometown of Pittsburgh, automation ideas were cubbyholed and the establishment restored an old-fashioned commuter rail service from downtown to the suburb of McKeesport some 20 miles away. This rail link managed to survive 15 years of deficit operations until it died a natural death in 1986. But this rail "channel" was very strong It kept the bureaucracy focused on conventional, old-fashioned rail transit. The establishment proceeded to build a non-automated, circa 1930 trolley car system (called Light Rail Transit) from downtown to the suburbs about 18 miles out. This new but already outdated system has never reached 40 percent of its forecasted patronage and the service declines gradually as payrolls increase and deficits rise.

This type of transit performance has sprawled all across the nation under the guise of "new technology." Each year UMTA introduces a catchword for a new activity in the coming fiscal year — Comprehensive Planning, Joint Development, Privatization, Public-private Partnerships, Suburban Mobility, New Directions etc. Last year they developed a National Conference on Regional Mobility in Phoenix, Arizona. The previous year beautiful areas surrounding Phoenix were the scene of a massive campaign to create a multi-billion dollar commuter rail system. Fortunately, it was turned down by the voters, but the process split the community apart. The regional mobility conference was not the answer; it was a political salve.

What's the problem? For one thing, we do not effectively audit our transit performance. Otherwise, why would we keep repeating the same mistakes in city after city? How could we designate the Miami and Detroit downtown people mover systems as successes in transit seminars long after they were obvious failures by any measure you choose.

The technology and equipment in the Detroit and Miami DPM systems were fine. But the patronage and financial performance have been atrocious because those systems were limited to just the circulation mission and were not integrated into developments. Most automobiles and buses already have driven into the city center and parked before their passengers have the opportunity to get onto the people movers.

Meanwhile the French in Lille are accomplishing the circulation without extra cost. Their two main automated guideway transit lines do not cross in the center of the city. Instead they create a circle in the downtown area. With this design they obtain a demand response and excellent patronage.

For the first time since I have been working in public transit a transit agency has been able to lure passengers out of their automobiles. In fact, 47 percent of the passengers in Lille are new to public transit.

We should analyze and directly compare our performance with the Lille system. And we must give them credit for their achievements, even if they are copying U.S. technology.

Comparing your product with your competitor's product is a common practice in manufacturing. At Westinghouse in the past we did it for many products, part by part. This "Competitive Cost Comparison" (C.C.C.) program was very successful in lowering product costs and improving quality.

### Let's Compare Transit Systems

Public transportation in America needs to do this sort of competitive comparison with the transit systems and development performance of other nations. One hears a lot of excuses for not doing so. "Europeans and Japanese are different." Absurd. They want the same speed, comfort and efficiency in their public transportation that everyone else does.

A second part of the problem is the urgent need to change our horizontal growth processes. In commercial and community development, we need to start planning public mobility from the inside and work outward. Up to now, it has been done in the opposite direction. We build a cluster of high-rise buildings near a highway or rail line, then circle or crisscross them with highways and a transit line of some sort. Highways come first, the transit thinking comes last.

Instead of this failed pattern, we must begin transit planning with the buildings themselves, starting at the top. Inside and through each building or commercial complex a transit system must be designed to move outward, as efficiently as from top to bottom, to the main transportation artery, be it highway or rail. We need growth from within, not transit from without.

Walt Disney became aware of this need. When I was working with him in planning transportation for EPCOT he bewailed the fact that his original Disneyland in California had quickly been surrounded outside its perimeter by commercial developers who eventually were making more money than he was from Disneyland operations. He vowed this would not happen to him at the new Walt Disney World.

Walt made a good start in Florida by buying some 28,000 acres and forming his own political district — a far greater area than the theme park itself would require. He was determined to control the perimeter development outside the park itself. But he underestimated the horizontal transportation system that would be created by the automobile. New highways and businesses grew for miles beyond his property, all depending on the popularity of Walt Disney World.

Were Walt alive today, I believe he would be repeating the same lament about Walt Disney World that he did about DisneyLand. "The developers are making more money on my investments than I am."

Well, almost anyway.

### Horizontal Development Process (HDP)
The relationship of horizontal development and public transit usually is carried out in isolated fashion. While in the vertical we account for every square foot, horizontally the land use is squandered, perhaps because we have so much.

My concern about the lack of attention to a more efficient horizontal growth process is what led to the study and creation of what is now termed the Horizontal Development Process (HDP).

From my experience that rainy afternoon on the BART line and many other subsequent observations, I knew that the idea of the transit "station" standing alone was no longer valid. Not only on the BART system was this true. Practically all conventional transit systems built in the past were designed to simply link stations, not take people to their ultimate destinations. By isolating the stations, security has become a serious problem on some of these systems. In New York City, for example, the transit station became an oasis in no man's land, requiring the largest transit police force ever and increasing fares even more.

It was clear to me that future transit systems, to be successful and attract patronage, had to take passengers where they want to go. . . to stores. . . to restaurants. . . to theaters. . . to hotels. . . to offices, not just to the next transit station. I was fascinated by what John Portman had done in Atlanta in the vertical dimension.

He created in the center of his Hyatt Regency Hotel an enormous atrium through which glass elevators rise and descend. (Fig. lB) Why not, I thought, lay this type of development on its side. Instead of the vertical elevator, install a horizontal elevator to carry the passenger from boutique to boutique, store to store, restaurant to hotel.

I had discussed these ideas not only with Bob Fairburn in Phoenix, but with Arch Rogers of RTKL in Baltimore, as well as John Portman, all past presidents of AIA. Their recommendations and encouragement led me to originate a logical approach that I call the Horizontal Development Process (HDP) and its Horizontal Elevator technology.

There are two distinct steps for implementation of an HDP project. The first is to plan and complete a concept, including the design. Second is to provide financial management aimed at optimizing the return on investment. This step separates conventional public transit from HDP. The Horizontal Development Process is made up of six components:

**Interception:** First, public transit must intercept the automobile which will remain the personal transportation mode for the foreseeable future. The system intercepts the automobile a short distance from the center of the city or other high density development and provides parking facilities at that point. The automobile driver and passengers park their car and step onto a "horizontal elevator."

Interception is the step which eliminates traffic congestion in the center of the high density area. This user-friendly interception also is applicable with suburban buses coming into the city. Buses lose much time in congested center city streets. Interception will actually increase bus patronage. It also will assist existing rail rapid transit lines to attract needed patronage.

**Horizontal Elevator:** This second component works just like a vertical elevator only it runs horizontally. It provides frequent, comfortable service and protection from the weather. It uses proven technology at reasonable cost. For the public, there is no waiting. A car comes every 55 to 72 seconds, 24 hours a day. There are no fare boxes, either. Did you ever have to pay a fare to ride a vertical elevator?

**Stopping Areas:** The third component is the stopping places — not transit stations but the places you want to go. The Horizontal Elevator takes you to a variety of stopping places where you can get off to shop, to dine, to see your dentist, to see a movie, or whatever. The vehicle runs right into these areas, letting you off in a pedestrian zone. Atriums can be created on the side of existing buildings. You get off inside the buildings. Here the pedestrian is king. Each stopping area adds business benefits. It is **not** a transit station. It is a marketable people area that produces income without requiring parking spaces or street access.

**Air Rights Developments:** The fourth component makes more growth possible without the limitations of street capacities or parking or zoning requirements. High-rise buildings can be built directly over the stopping areas and development can take place underneath. People can work there with new convenience. Expensive highway construction to the new buildings is rendered unnecessary.

**Entirely New Developments:** A fifth element made available through HDP is the opportunity to develop areas not usually available to developers — land which due to size, configuration or terrain could not accommodate a highway system. Inaccessible land is made accessible. The Horizontal Elevator will pass through land which is relatively undeveloped even in the center city. It provides opportunity to retrieve land values which have been passed over due to city street and irregular downtown development.

HDP also can provide a convenient mix of businesses and people activities. In today's community, some areas now tend to be all offices, or all retail stores, or all health or educational institutions. With HDP a blend of activities is made available. The Horizontal Elevator will move the passenger from one to another just as though they were located on different floors of the same high-rise building.

If these activities have a good marketing relationship they will generate profit and foster new growth. The so-called Edge Cities miss out on marketing potential because of too heavy concentration on offices and lack of community functions and human services.

**The Business Component:** A sixth and vital element of the new horizontal development approach is the management or business component, providing continuous financial management and planning for growth and profit. This management element designs, constructs, operates and maintains the corridor developments. Development space at each stopping area and the intercept parking can include the cost of the Horizontal Elevator as part of the rental fees. In Lille, France, to pay for the transit system, private employers (of more than nine people) agreed to a progressive assessment starting at one-half percent of payroll and moving to 1 1/2 percent. This provides funding equivalent to what our transit agencies obtain from federal and state contributions.

These six components have to be fitted to the increment of transit development being planned, but HDP can be a helpful guide to assuring maximum benefit from the transit investment.

Circus-Circus Enterprises in Las Vegas recognized the value of HDP when they faced the need to expand their facilities. They passed over an adjoining piece of land right on the strip priced at about $30 million and bought land back two blocks for near $6 million. On this land they were able to erect a higher, 32-story addition. To access this new property, they built an $8 million Horizontal Elevator (Fig. 9C). This strategy has resulted in profitable operations and has attracted more customers.

### Streets For People
One by-product of the HDP will be the chance to return some of our city streets to the pedestrian. In America today, the streets all belong to the automobile. The pedestrian comes in a poor second. This must change.

The center of the city should be the most used and the most valuable land for development. In a sense, we have closed it down, But it can be restored.

Closing several principal streets in the center of a city not only is possible but desirable. It will provide valuable "new land" in the most exciting location of a city when planning is centered on people and vehicles are intercepted. Intercepting vehicles is the secret. A number of cities already have done this successfully.

I received my first indoctrination on "streets for people" in 1964 when I visited my ancestral country of Sweden. In Vallingby, I was shown one of the first "multifunctional centers" in Europe with a large pedestrian area previously used for vehicular traffic. This was to have a great influence over my efforts during the next 25 years to improve mobility in the transit industry.

A subway was built from Stockholm out into the suburbs, under many towns including Vallingby. The Vallingby planners opted for a central area free of traffic. Automobiles and bicycles were restricted to the periphery. Seven functions were planned for the central area — a shopping mall, schools, churches, recreation, hotel, hospital and offices. The central area was planted with trees and flowers. Sidewalk cafes were introduced.

My next exposure to streets-for-people was in Munich, Germany in 1966. Downtown traffic had become unbearable in that old city. The city fathers decided to increase the commercial appeal downtown by making the main corridor of streets "pedestrian only." Deliveries could be made in certain hours and intercept parking garages were located at the ends of several streets which led into the walking area.

A hole was created right in front of the city hall on the walking street to provide access to a fine public transit system. Net result of the intercept garage and easy access — many more people coming downtown every day.

I observed and photographed the first year results and found the experiment to be quite successful. In the years that followed, the number of streets restricted to pedestrians has expanded (Figs. 10A, 10B, 10C, 10D). Some businesses objected when their location was not on the pedestrian area and they were compensated by lower rents and fees. They eventually became good members of the private organization which manages all functions of the pedestrian streets.

The streets-for-people idea continued to spread. Gothenburg, Sweden became another experimental laboratory and I received a copy of the planning for the Gothenburg Traffic Restraint scheme. The system was inaugurated in August, 1970. When I visited the city in 1971, I was amazed by what had been accomplished.

In Gothenburg, the scheme divides downtown into five zones, any one of which an automobile may enter but not pass through. One street was covered with a skylight structure, and others were soon to get roofs. In several years they created an exciting new Mall in this way. (Figs. 11A, 11B, 11C, 11D).

Today there are four covered streets which form a cross and the process is still growing. Along these streets are offices, a hotel, restaurants and shops.

On one of my trips to Gothenburg I noticed they had constructed one of the first large "intercept" parking garages just beyond one of the covered "walking" streets. It was raining and I got wet getting to this garage, so I suggested they open the wall and showcase window in the middle of the covered street. This way people could walk directly into the garage from the covered area without getting wet and probably would buy from the shops through which they walked.

There was no comment to my suggestion, but when I was there the following year I saw that all of the walls up and down all four covered streets had been removed (Figs. 11C, 11D). People now walked freely through the businesses located in the covered area — and many more people were coming downtown throughout the day and evening.

Many towns and cities in recent years have revived their central areas. The process of regrowing this high density land is ideally suitable for the Horizontal Development Process.

Most city officials and planners believe their central areas are full — no more room for growth. But this is not so. HDP will make room for **people activities** while increasing the capacity of the central city for additional growth. It also will reduce air pollution from auto emissions, enabling cities to meet the Clean Air Act amendment standards which take effect in 1995. Failure to meet those standards could bring mandatory restrictions on auto travel in the central areas.

The six steps of HDP, coupled with excellence in private development, will bring increased business with less congestion to the center city and also return joy and excitement to an area that once was the heart of America's growth.

# CHAPTER TWELVE

# The Technology Worshippers

We "worship" new technology. Never mind if it will work and provide the best overall performance in a particular situation. If the technology is new and fascinating, we go for it hook, line and semiconductor. And we go for it hardest if it's being introduced someplace far, far away.

Think how often Congressmen go on junkets to Europe or the Far East and come home announcing that the latest technology they saw there is "the answer" to America's transportation problems. They did it when they first rode the Japanese bullet trains. They did it when they saw magnetic levitation demonstrated in Germany. And I'll bet that, in 218 B.C., when Hannibal moved his Carthaginian Army across the Alps using elephants, a dozen "experts" in Rome and Greece said "there's the answer to our transportation problems." Something accomplished a long way from home is always more intriguing than something done in our own backyard.

You need only review the history of the greatest transportation invention of our time — the airplane — to discover that the same thing happened in America then.

When the two Dayton, Ohio boys, Wilbur and Orville Wright, successfully achieved the first powered flight in 1903 on the sand dunes of Kitty Hawk, N.C., they had a terrible time getting America to pay any attention to their historic achievement. Even the Dayton newspapers gave very little space to the story. The local editors weren't even tempted by the "local boys make good" angle. And when the Wrights continued to carry on their test flights on "Huffman prairie" — a piece of farmland eight miles outside of town — few people paid any attention. The Dayton papers didn't even send a reporter out to watch.

Sensing a possible military application in their invention, the Wrights prepared a proposal to the U.S. Secretary of War, sending it through their local Congressman. Their proposal, however, was routed through War Department channels and resulted in a stock reply indicating little interest. Several other approaches were made with equally negative results. Who was it that first showed real interest? From several thousand miles away, it was the French.

As related in Fred Howard's biography on the Wright Brothers, "Wilbur and Orville," a representative of a syndicate of French businessmen arrived in Dayton during Christmas week of 1905. He negotiated a contract with the Wrights which gave his group an option to buy a Wright Flyer if certain terms were met.

It was only after news of the strong French interest reached Washington, that the U.S. government woke up and began to play "catch-up ball" in seeking to acquire rights to the new technology.

It isn't surprising that France was one of the first nations to take the new aviation technology seriously. The French always have taken a fancy to new technology. They did so when the U.S. developed a new energy technology — nuclear power. France today produces 70 percent of its electricity using that technology, leading the world in that regard by far. Seventy-eight of its 82 nuclear plants are of the Westinghouse PWR design. France also is a leader in the application — if not the invention — of new transportation technologies — people movers and high speed trains are two examples. The former was developed first in America and the latter in Japan.

### Apply It, Don't Worship It.

The big mistake we and others sometimes make is that we are dazzled by the technology and pay too little attention to its total application. Technology is only one factor in solving a complex problem in our society. It is not to be worshipped. It's to be **applied**, and applied in the most cost efficient manner possible. That's the bottom line. The **total system** is the thing. Too often we study the technology but fail to audit the performance of the total system of which it is a part. Even the French have fallen victim to this.

In 1968 I was invited to visit a new jet engine transit project in France. You probably never heard of it. But they could sure hear it in France. This test line ran from south of Paris 12 miles to Joan of Arc's hometown of Orleans. It was intended to show how airplane technology could be applied to ground transit and achieve very high speeds. The company developing the system wanted to license Westinghouse to sell it in America. That's why I was there.

I was treated to a 150 miles-per-hour ride in a vehicle that resembled a Boeing 707 on wheels. Inside the vehicle, the ride was very impressive. Smooth and fast. Then I got out and stood beside the guideway while the train passed by at that high speed. Well, the noise from the jet engine was absolutely deafening. Where, I thought, could such a system be installed? Certainly not near my home. The French government, fascinated by the jet engine technology, had invested millions of francs in this system without ever considering the total impact of the system on its surroundings. Single point verification, I call that. Needless to say, that project died shortly after our visit when the French finally got around to evaluating the total system.

So it goes as each new technology emerges. We hear statements such as: "PRT is the answer for transit in our cities;" or "LRT will solve our traffic problems;" or "AGT will save our cities;" or "America is losing the Maglev race;" or "Super Trains are solutions to America's transportation gridlock."

None of these statements is true because no one of these technologies is **the** answer. Unless they are applied properly and integrated into systems that move people where they want to go, they all will fail to solve the problem of greater public mobility in our cities.

Let's take a look at some of the new technologies now being proposed or used in the effort to solve our local or regional transit problems.

### PRT — Personalized Rapid Transit
Starting with the smallest unit capacity type system is PRT, or Personalized Rapid Transit. This would provide vehicles carrying from two to eight passengers each which would travel all around a city. Providing a personalized service to meet the needs of the individual, this sounded appealing until a good analysis was made.

Dr. D.H. Maund of Ford Motor Company made a technical evaluation of all factors involved in the application of such a system and found, not to our surprise, that the smaller the vehicle, the higher the cost per unit of trip generation. Furthermore, guideways erected all over a city would prove unsightly and enormously expensive in a downtown environment.

The best known PRT system actually to be installed is the one at West Virginia University in Morgantown, W.Va. In 1972, Dr. Sam Elias initiated a study for a PRT system to connect remote campus locations and downtown Morgantown. Predicted to cost $18 million, costs soared to more than $100 million with federal government funding. Then a $67 million addition was recommended to solve problems which became apparent.

As an example of how these problems were "solved," a link was added to reach the medical school. The **station** for the medical school stop was located on the side of a nearby hill. To reach the medical school, the passengers must walk up a flight of uncovered stairs, then cross a large parking lot, then cross a street, being careful to avoid the bus which has just let its passengers off at the medical school's front door! Who called this "personalized" service? The bus gives better service for a lower fare.

This PRT system won Senator William Proxmire's "Golden Fleece" award and the *Readers Digest* reported on this system in an article titled "Anatomy of a Boondogle."

Perhaps the worst part of this scheme was that it took about five acres of the most valuable ground in the center of the campus — where level land is at a premium — and erected there a transfer station. All cost and little productive benefit.

What did they do at Morgantown? They tried to insert a new transit technology into a 1900 conventional transit system design. Needless to say, the world has not judged this system to be an answer to its modern transit problems. Every once in a while PRT is resuscitated because it appears to serve all the needs of the individual. But when analysis discloses the cost and physical displacement in a central city, the projects become overwhelming.

### LRT — Light Rail Transit
LRT, light rail transit, was born after we spent billions on the new, high tech subway/elevated systems in San Francisco, Atlanta and Miami which I described in Chapter Nine. Something cheaper had to be found.

This is a modernized and streamlined version of the rail trolley systems of the 1920s. The cars run quieter and smoother than the old trolleys and are more comfortable inside, but they still require a motorman up front and simply link transit stations. There are 10 such LRT systems in U.S. cities, all suffering from escalating costs and lower than expected ridership. Their low performance will be something those cities must live with into the 21st century (Table 1, Pg. 31).

These LRT systems are examples of single point verification —they cost less than the rail subway systems like BART or MARTA, but, not being integrated into the commercial life and developments of the cities, they fail to offer the total system performance that people will demand if they are to depend on public transit. The graph on page 72 shows the poor record of U.S. conventional transit ridership.

## Maglev — Magnetic Levitation

This technology uses the phenomenon of electromagnetism to lift the transit vehicles just above the roadbed as they are powered along at up to 300 miles per hour.

My experience with this dates back to 1968 when Allan S. Boyd, the newly-appointed first Secretary of Transportation, came to Pittsburgh to address our Third International Conference on Urban Transportation.

I picked him up at the airport in a helicopter so he could quickly get to the first fully automated transit system at the South Park demonstration site. After he rode that system, we whirled him over to the Westinghouse Research Laboratories a few miles away to witness the magnetic transit experiment.

We had just finished there a year's work on a 20-foot-long guideway over which a vehicle was levitated. After Boyd took his short demonstration ride he was presented with a certificate affirming that he had been levitated in space above the earth in one of the first magnetic transit experiments.

As a result of our work on magnetic support systems, however, we made the decision to discontinue the program. Today, even though there is much "worship" of this technology in some circles, I believe our decision was correct.

This is an exciting technology, of course. A transit vehicle without wheels riding on magnets attracts the imagination of the would-be transit experts, especially political leaders. Elimination of wheel wear and its friction, the potential of less energy required and the highest speed ground transit yet demonstrated are some of the impressive features. But is that the total story?

Both Germany and Japan have invested a great deal of money in magnetic systems development. They both have demonstrated physical feasibility at very high speeds for ground transportation. One short, medium speed, two-mile system was operating as an add-on to the Berlin Metro Transit System, but it has been torn down and replaced with a conventional system. A Maglev system was started and abandoned at Las Vegas. A consortium using the German Transrapid Maglev system expects to build a 14-mile line between the edge of Walt Disney World and Orlando International Airport in Florida.

In my opinion, the value of the magnetic support technology has yet to be proven commercially. There is no commercial Maglev system installed at this writing. It requires a whole new propulsion system, such as a linear motor, to drive the vehicle and it may never prove to be cost competitive with other transit technologies on short city systems.

But the lure of new technology is strong. A group of 12 corporations in the Pittsburgh area have established a project to build a Maglev system 19 miles long from downtown to the Pittsburgh International Airport.

These companies organized the project around the high speed railroad department at Carnegie Mellon University with Dick Uher as director. Uher is a former employee of the Westinghouse Transportation Division. The objective of this group is not only to construct a transit system to the airport, but to bring the new magnetic levitation manufacturing to Pittsburgh. A group of Japanese banks planned to contribute $250,000 to the project in the form of loans.

This project may have received its death blow, however, when $700 million approved for Maglev by Congress was included in a $103 billion package of federal spending cuts endorsed by the House of Representatives in late October, 1993.

Unfortunately, technology — no matter how fascinating —doesn't guarantee success. Several studies have been made over the past 20 years on carrying people from downtown Pittsburgh to the airport. None of these studies has ever predicted adequate patronage to support a conventional transit system for this single purpose. Just changing the technology will not enable such a transit line to support the tremendous investment —unless a new approach is taken to the route and mission of the system. This project is dubious at best, lacking an adequate market.

If the Maglev system is so quiet it can access directly into buildings like a horizontal elevator, and if private developers are brought into the planning early on, it could have a chance. But a conventional approach that simply links transit stations following an old railroad right-of-way is questionable at best.

Magnetic Levitation has one outstanding advantage. It is the only ground system capable of safe travel at 300 mph or more. But how do you take advantage of traveling at such speed? It requires long distances to get up to speed and then slow down. At such speeds, station stops would be few and far between. Track layout would require straight lines and few if any curves or tunnels. In the proposed Pittsburgh application, it would not be possible for the Maglev train to reach more than 100 miles an hour (a third of its speed capability) at any point along the expected route.

To apply Maglev successfully requires a total analysis of all factors, including total cost, reliability, physical limitations, marketability and growth potential.

The jury is still out on Maglev.

## *High Speed Rail — The "Super Trains"*

There is a fine success story in this technology. High speed rail is a profitable, exciting way to carry large numbers of people between cities. It can have an important role in our total transportation scheme of things. But it is being over-sold as a "solution to America's transportation gridlock."

First let's examine what it is.

The man who deserves the most credit for the success of high speed rail is my old friend Dr. Shima, who still is working as a senior advisor to the Japanese National Space Agency as of this writing. His work on creating the first railroad system to operate at more than 150 miles per hour in frequent, daily and competitive service has been recognized around the world. He has received high honors from France, England and his own country, among others.

Dr. Shima did not introduce any radically new technology. His forte was to apply excellent engineering practices to an entire system. He engineered every component — locomotives, cars, wheels, motors, catenaries, tracks, roadbeds and all other details — to peak efficiency. Unifying all these items, Dr. Shima showed the world how to achieve excellence.

Anyone could readily see how to accomplish the same result, but only two countries, so far, have done it. They are France and Germany. The French TGV trains now travel up to 186 miles per hour. The German ICE trains travel at over 160 m.p.h. There is little doubt that these systems evolved from the knowledge created in Japan.

The first Japanese Shinkansen, "bullet train," line (Fig. 13A) was built from Tokyo to Osaka, about 300 miles, between 1958 and 1964. This New Tokaido line stole much of the passenger business from the airlines and began to generate a profit in its second year of operation.

I learned some little known facts about this story when the Shima family resided in our home for a short time in the 1960s.

In the late '50s, there had been a train wreck in Japan not unlike the one that occurred on the Penn Central Railroad outside Philadelphia, killing about the same number of people — 200. Dr. Shima was chief engineer of the Japan National Railroad at that time and he was forced to resign.

When the Japanese decided to build a new high-speed rail system in 1960, they recalled Dr. Shima. He was the only man they considered capable of getting that big job done successfully. Mrs. Shima told me that the day JNR recalled her husband, thus vindicating him of the rail disaster, was "happy day my life," as she said it in her limited English.

The Japanese continue to improve on this system. In 1988 I was invited to take a ride on the second generation of the high speed Shinkansen (Fig. 13B) from Tokyo to Osaka by Tak Shima, son of Dr. Shima. He walked me along the train and stopped in the center. I was aware that he wanted me to observe something.

When I looked up, I was surprised to see that the central cars of the train were double-decked. Then we went inside. The upstairs deck was super first class, nicer than the first class section of any airliner I had ever seen. Large, wide windows, soft adjustable seats, a hostess moving around with beverages, snacks and magazines. TV and weather reports.

Downstairs were compartments for three or four people equipped with telephones and computer modems. You could work there in comfort and contact your home office via computer all the way to Osaka.

The speed of these second generation bullet trains has been increased from 150 to 180 miles per hour and special dining cars have been added. Tak told me that three trains already were in operation, sold out for months in advance. JNR, the Japanese National Railway, now was simply JR — a private venture and making a profit.

The Japanese high speed trains are an excellent example of how to apply existing technology in the development of excellence in service which will grow and earn a profit. It is not the high speed technology alone that does the job. It is the way they package the total system to meet the traveler's needs.

The French lost little time in pursuing the Japanese high speed train technology. Their original TGV (Trés Grande Vitesse) line from Paris to Lyon, built from 1972 to 1981, was followed in 1989 by the TGV Atlantique line from Paris to LeMans. Traveling at 186 miles per hour, the TGV trains on this line were called the "world's fastest." Also in 1989 the French announced plans to extend the Paris-Lyon line southeast to the Winter Olympic sites and Grenoble by 1992, and on to Valence two years later.

These new TGV 10-car trains are powered by front and rear electric locomotives that run on 25,000 volts, generating 12,000 horsepower. They are 40 percent more powerful than the original TGVs.

France is planning an entire TGV network and hopes to extend it to other countries. Germany is planning a similar approach with their ICE trains and Sweden with their #2000 trains. New high speed rail lines are being built in France and Belgium to link their capitals with the new 31-mile "chunnel" being constructed beneath the English Channel. BritRail also is investing $1.1 billion to upgrade rails and signaling equipment and complete a new international rail terminal in London which is to be connected to the "chunnel." A fleet of 30 new trains is being built.

America still does not have a successful application of high speed rail technology. The limiting factor has been our inability to bring everything together, politically, technically, financially. Thus far we have lacked the experienced leadership to package a competitive system of ground transportation. Hoping to change this, a Texas group announced in mid-1991 plans to build a 620-mile TGV system linking Dallas, Houston, San Antonio, Austin and Fort Worth. However, lack of financing now appears to have derailed this project.

That's high speed rail as it stands today. In the next chapter we'll examine its potential or limitations for helping improve mobility in our cities and airports.

### AGT — Automated Guideway Transit

We've already talked about Automated Guideway Transit but a further word is in order. AGT has not yet been properly applied to achieve its maximum potential. The experience of Lille, France and three systems in Japan are only the first phase in the application of the automated system. Further increases in mobility will be achieved when this transit technology is better integrated into commercial development.

The horizontal elevator concept needs to closely follow the lead of vertical elevator systems, with high performance in the total picture of costs, convenience, trip times, marketability and excitement. I believe architects and private developers will insist on such evaluation. We need the same approach to transit mobility in the horizontal realm as we have had in the vertical.

Automation, of course, is the key to improved safety whether applied to machinery or vehicles. Operator error is eliminated. And operator error is by far the most frequent cause of transportation accidents. Automated systems do have failures due to inadequate maintenance or failed components, but sequential means of fail safe design enable such systems to continue operating safely.

From 1970 when eight AGT people movers went into operation at the Tampa

International Airport until 1990, automated systems of this type carried over 60 million passengers without a single fatality. Now such systems are being installed worldwide.

## The Future of Transit Technology
The greatest shortcoming in existing applications of new transit technology is that almost all have been installed as part of conventional transit systems of the 1900s. This is the result of employing the traditional transit agencies and consultants who, in my mind, do not have the benefit of corporate research capability.

Even when such transit people obtain research grants from the government, they depend primarily on "proven technology" from the past. They design transit stations, fare collection systems, traditional access and egress methods — all the existing impediments of the old line transit systems that are failing to solve our traffic problems of today.

Just as our generals often are accused of preparing to "fight the last war over again," so our transit consultants are trying to solve tomorrow's transit problems with yesterday's methods.

To improve public mobility in the next century, we must take the privatization portion of the planning out of the hands of the transit agencies and consultants and put it in the hands of the imaginative architects and developers who are beginning to understand that mobility holds the key to their commercial success in the future. And the place to begin is with incremental intercept systems and horizontally planned connections.

# CHAPTER THIRTEEN

# Can "Super Trains" Improve Urban Mobility?

Much confusion exists in the public mind on the relationship of urban public transit to the long haul, high speed rail systems. Some people, I'm sure, believe the solution to traffic gridlock in our cities is to criss-cross the U.S. with high speed trains as in Europe and Japan.

We had similar misconceptions back in the 1960s about rail rapid transit. It was supposed to eliminate traffic congestion and the motorist would leave his vehicle at home.

Cities now have received transit funding for the next six years amounting to $151 billion for all modes. Called ISTEA (iced tea) legislation, it stands for the Intermodal Surface Transportation Efficiency Act. And voices are being heard in many states urging that most of that money be spent to install high speed rail systems that will solve the ground transportation congestion once and for all.

Is this to be the new syndrome of Congress for solving our mobility problems? Where's the intermodal efficiency? Where's development?

Unfortunately the politicians now see sudden political opportunity in high speed rail. It's a new technology bandwagon to climb on. . . and big contracts to be won for their constituents. So the super train is being touted as the answer to America's transportation problems. But slow down! It's just one part of an answer. And it isn't an answer at all unless we approach it the right way.

High speed rail is not a thing unto itself. A wonderful system when properly used, the high cost super train can work **only if the marketplace supports it**. How different was the marketing situation for the early railroads in the late 19th and early 20th centuries. They really didn't have a market problem, nor did they have regulatory problems.

The early railroad owners had complete freedom to build as they wanted. They had low cost land which could be used freely. There was the right of eminent domain, no environmental restrictions, liberal tax laws and generous subsidies. And wherever the railroaders built their stations, communities grew up to supply the market.

No wonder great fortunes were made in early railroading!

But the planners of the high speed rail lines today have serious problems — land availability, environmental restrictions, technical problems, and, above all, assurance of a strong market at both ends of each high speed rail link. Today the potential market is sprawled across the countryside, wherever the automobile and highway network reaches.

The high speed rail technology is costly to purchase and even more so to maintain. The right-of-way required is very expensive because of the need for long stretches of straight track.

High speed systems can help America solve its urban traffic congestion problems, but not if they are installed as railroads were. They must be integrated into the nation's overall transportation network and above all into the urban transit systems of those cities they will serve, as France is doing with the TGV at Lille. That's where their markets must be found.

### What High Speed Rail Is Not
We saw in the previous chapter what high speed rail **is.** But it is necessary also to examine what it is **not.**

An example of how people misunderstand the potential of high speed rail was supplied some time ago by humorist Andy Rooney. In his newspaper column he waxed eloquently about an exciting ride he had had on a French TGV Atlantique train which reached 186 miles-an-hour. And he compared this with his experience making frequent journeys from New York to Albany by both automobile and airplane.

The auto trip, he said, takes him about three hours. The next time he took the plane he timed it. With the traffic delays getting to LaGuardia and landing delays at Albany, the trip took four hours and 21 minutes. How wonderful it would be, he wrote, to take the French super train which would make the trip in 48 minutes!

Andy is a good writer but he's no transportation engineer. Obviously, he took the TGV 186 mph top speed and divided it into the 150 mile distance. And he came up with a 48-minute elapsed time for the trip.

I wrote Andy a letter pointing out that on his proposed super train trip to Albany he would have to leap off the train at his destination while it was going 186 mph. Some leap! And the trip would have to accelerate at the start from zero to 186 almost instantly. Some whip lash! High speed trains would find it impossible to go from NYC to Albany in 48 minutes, or anything close to it.

The bullet train in Japan takes many miles to slow down to a stop from a speed of 180 miles an hour. And to reach its top speed at the beginning of a run takes at least 5 to 10 miles depending on track conditions. So, in reality, Andy's trip from New York to Albany now averages about 130 miles an hour, not 186. And what about the roadbed and curves that will affect the high speed performance negatively?

Not long ago, I read a new book on super trains which called them "solutions to America's transportation gridlock." The well-illustrated volume described the French, Japanese and U.S. high speed rail projects, as well as others being planned in the world. It is a fine inventory of technology. But nowhere did I find any explanation of how the super trains will solve America's traffic gridlock problems.

### Ready Access To Urban Centers Is A Key
Traffic congestion in our urban areas will not be solved just by adding new rail lines, be they fast or slow. The problem is much too complex for that. It is conceivable, in fact, that the super trains could make traffic congestion in our cities **worse** rather than better. The areas around railroad stations are known for their traffic complexity. And when the new super trains dump their passenger loads into the city, the traffic congestion will grow proportionately unless by that time there exists an innovative access system to carry all of those people where they want to go.

In other words, we must have greatly improved access to our cities and much higher quality of transit performance at competitive prices. Super trains must be coupled with modern public transit systems that are integrated into people activities in the cities.

The newest TGV interchange in Lille, France is an excellent example of such integration. This location includes a number of private developments such as food service in addition to the large passenger interchange area. The TGV trains pass right through the building, providing access for its passengers to the best rapid transit system in the world and direct connections to two nearby cities. It is truly a center for a Eurorail system. Here you are provided direct connections to Paris and London almost every hour, non-stop. The TGV trains are one of the two rail lines permitted to continue right through the Chunnel under the English Channel to England. This Lille interchange is certainly **not** a conventional railroad station.

There also is an excellent example of integrating trains with other modes of transportation that has been instituted by Lufthansa in Germany — the Lufthansa Airport Express. At the Frankfurt Airport terminal, international and domestic arriving passengers can continue "their flight" on a moderate speed train (125 mph as of now) to Cologne, Bonn and Stuttgart. And when Lufthansa says "continue your flight" they mean just that. The airline attendants, meals, baggage handling and other flight services are provided on the trains which usually run four times a day. For airline passengers, this eliminates many short haul flights and brings them right downtown at their destination.

These trains already have had a measurable effect on the traffic congestion, not only in the air but also on the ground, freeing up space for urgently needed gates and reducing the number of cars parking at the airport. The number of short haul trips by air also is reduced. So here indeed is one example of improved rail service reducing traffic congestion around a major city airport, if not in the city itself.

In tackling traffic congestion we are facing a big selling job. We must attract ridership away from a familiar transportation system that is private and is immediately available 24 hours a day; one that is not limited to a narrow path or track and which will carry baggage conveniently. Yes, the automobile is a tough transportation system to beat — except for one big weakness. More and more, the driver and his passengers are sitting in long bumper-to-bumper lines in our urban areas, going nowhere.

But it is amazing how bad traffic congestion can become before people will object to "parking" on the highway and waiting for interminable periods. Also, the cost of parking the car in the city has risen astronomically. Some downtown buildings in New York City charge more than $30 a day. The average American driver is about at the end of his rope paying $10 to $15 a day, or $2,000 to $3,000 a year, just to park his car.

### *Tracks and Roadbeds*

In addition to requiring high quality access to the center city, the super trains have other problems to overcome. Rights of way. Existing tracks and roadbeds are not equal to the high speed task.

While ordinary rail transit is applicable to systems as short as 15 or 20 miles, high speed rail requires 200 to 300 mile distances to be practical and economical. Frequent station stops are out. Japan's bullet trains between Tokyo and Osaka stop only once in the more than 200-mile run.

Trains going at 200 mph plus speeds will require absolutely straight track for long distances. Curves are to be avoided. If a train has to slow down for many curves, or for station stops, you might as well install a much lower cost and slower but well-engineered rail system.

The planners in Texas intend to employ the French TGV highly-engineered, conventional railroad. They found that costs and questions about the magnetic, higher-speed systems have not yet been answered.

The high speed systems must have better roadbeds than now exist in the U.S. There must be critical control of the distance from the track to the pantograph that touches the overhead cantenary. While the safety record of international super trains is excellent, this does not assure the same performance in this country. Magnetic track must be inspected every night and maintained to a close tolerance of flatness. The bullet train tracks in Japan, for example, are inspected every night by sophisticated equipment. Adjustments are made automatically.

If we set out simply to match the present performance of the transit and high speed rail systems in France and Japan, we will again find ourselves behind the parade in another 10 years. We have the opportunity to learn from our competition and **better** their performance.

To make the high-speed rail systems economically feasible, there must be markets at both ends of each high speed link. We do have many good corridors for high speed rail in the U.S. but there must be imaginative planning and development. For example, the developers of the proposed high speed project in Florida defined their corridors well, but they could not get their markets lined up to include sufficient land developments and people involvement.

The Japanese, French and Germans have the markets and developments in good focus so local trains have to operate every 15 to 30 minutes to meet demand.

There are a great number of qualified developers, architects and entrepreneurs in America to create the profitable interfaces of public transit and high-speed rail. Only when these systems are easily accessible to each other and integrated with people activities will a true "service demand" be created.

### Superior Corridor Development Essential

How can high-speed rail succeed in America? Only by insisting on truly superior corridor development. Super trains operating from Boston, New York, Philadelphia and Washington will only be a reality when they are planned and implemented on a world class basis. And this will require three steps:

Step One, ACCESS to the centers and suburbs of the city. This means effective use of the AGT "horizontal elevator" technology — to carry people where they want to go with service at least every 55 seconds. On my last trip to Lille, France, I timed trains leaving the station at the end of the line every 45 seconds!

Step Two, PRIVATE DEVELOPMENT at each major city stopping point. Conventional train stations do not generate sufficient market or continued growth. Developments should contain a marketable mix of financial, educational, health, recreational and general businesses.

Step Three, SCOPE large enough and important enough to attract the international development world. These super train stops must be **important places**, not just places to get on or off the train. Each major city stopping place should be a showplace —privately organized in a first class manner with profit providing the incentive. A minimum of three or as many as five developers ought to plan the developments at each area and create the market for growth.

Financing can be a blend of public and private. The rights-of-way can be furnished by the public sector, just as highways are supplied for automobile use. The trains, rails and equipment, including system operation, can be supplied by the private developers as part of their profit-making businesses.

The Japanese high-speed rail systems now are private, and innovation is increasing passenger demand. Double-decker cars, higher speeds and more frequent service are building patronage.

When private developers are involved they do need help, but the separation between public and private must be clean. If the private developer does not make a profit he soon disappears from the scene. The best example of the separation required can be found in large high-rise building complexes. The private developers' architects design their own vertical transportation systems.

The key to making the super trains work to reduce urban area traffic congestion is to integrate them with new urban center access designs. The Lufthansa Airport Express is one good example of integrating air and rail systems. Another is the new Roissypole development at Charles DeGaulle international airport. There the new TGV trains will connect with the RER high speed transit into Paris, amidst a modern airport that will handle 200 million passengers by the year 2,000 — great accessibility by multiple modes of transportation.

It is only when high-speed rail and transit are planned in concert that gridlock can be conquered. The Euralille TGV and Metro complex is another excellent example, of course.

To promote super trains effectively in the U.S. there must be some integration of the federal bureaucracy in the Department of Transportation. Today there is little integration of planning among air, rail, transit and highway. Attempts to solve traffic congestion usually result in adding more highways.

Some overview organization should be formed, drawing from each of the transportation agencies — FAA, FHA, FTA and FRA — to achieve integrated planning and action. This group should consider development of improved methods of moving people without the restraints of existing vehicle systems. Walt Disney integrated the monorail transit with hotel, restaurant, shops and recreation. Lufthansa has broken the barrier between railroad and airplane. The transportation system in John Portman's hotel joins five businesses in a vertical alignment. This kind of thinking is needed to break away from the strait jacket of past practices. People must be given priority over vehicles and vehicle systems.

Our federal bureaucracy needs to look forward not backward and take us to a higher level of integrated mobility. Fortunately, we do not have to wait for new technology. Much is available, waiting to be applied.

# CHAPTER FOURTEEN

# Returning The City To People

Our city planners have done a fine job of making room in our cities for everything but people. They have carved out highways and cloverleaves, tunneled conventional transit into the city centers, high rise buildings abound, parking garages cover large acreage.

As these cities grew, what has happened? The city center has become a collection of business towers and congestion where people are seen commuting to and from work, period. The people-centered activities have gotten crowded out.

In Pittsburgh, for example, Fifth Avenue used to be the spine down the center of the Golden Triangle, providing people with many kinds of commercial, specialized retail and recreational activities. No more. The specialized shops, a theater and restaurants are gone. People move up and down the forlorn street mainly to get somewhere else.

As the downtown businesses wanted to expand, they moved to the suburbs where they created limited function, high-density areas now being called Edge Cities. As much as possible they emphasized least possible expense to the developers. Transit was supplied by the automobile backed by highway funding.

What will it take to bring people back into the city centers and put fun and entertainment back into the city? It will take **vision** in planning.

In the opening chapter we discussed the essential elements needed to improve the mobility of the American people. The first of these was vision.

Without vision, leadership goes nowhere. And that's been our main problem for decades in public transit. We have been led by people who have offered conventional answers — with requests for more money — to solve problems which defy the conventional —problems that demand vision.

The result has been the deterioration of our urban centers caused by the inability of people to move about easily, comfortably and economically. So now we have the Edge Cities to contend with... the clusters of business activities on the edge of town which lack the heart and soul — the community quality — of the old city.

We must avoid the conclusion that the Edge City will replace the old city. Fortunately for America, this need not be so.

Aside from its beautiful land and rich resources, America's greatest assets are its cities. They house our educational and cultural centers, our seats of government, our hubs of commerce, important social and recreational facilities. But most of these cities have been in decline for years. They have been allowed to deteriorate mainly because they lack public mobility.

It has become simply too hard, tiresome and time-consuming to get around in our downtown areas anymore. So men and women of vision have been abandoning the downtown and moving their activities out to the suburbs. The shopping malls are replacing the great downtown department stores. The sports stadium gets built miles outside of town.

But this is proving to be a temporary solution at best. We now are finding that the urban congestion is moving to the suburban areas also. As they grow bigger, they are inheriting the same mobility problems that are found downtown. Places like Tysons Corner, VA, Upper Merion, PA, Century City, CA and similar places are beginning to suffer problems similar to those of the older cities, and without the benefits of retrofitting and reclaiming the wonderful scenes and events of the past. The Edge Cities lack community spirit and people events.

The Horizontal Development Process has been designed to improve that situation and make possible the turnaround necessary to accomplish incremental projects. The process we are developing will be just as valuable to the Edge Cities as to urban centers. They depend on automobile travel and can be spared the inevitable center congestion by the same methods as downtown.

What we must do is obvious. **We must save our great cities!** It is not only foolish but economically impossible to abandon them. As the nation's population continues to rise, our cities will continue to grow and the cost will continue to rise. Someone must pay it.

## Vision With HDP
Fortunately, with vision in the application of HDP, our cities **can** be saved!

Where can we look for visionary leadership in this vital effort? We must look to the people who have been demonstrating the most innovative and imaginative thinking — the private developers who have been creating our suburban centers. Look to them to be creative not only in constructing imaginative buildings, but also in providing people mobility which is the secret to urban salvation.

Who are such leaders? They are people like John Portman, developer of the glass elevator and atrium in Atlanta; like Walt Disney who built the monorail right into the lobby of his Contemporary Hotel in Florida; like Leigh Fisher at Tampa International where 10 horizontal elevators shuttle people quickly and easily within that great airport. It will be such people, leaders with vision, who will provide the leadership in planning urban development for the years ahead.

To such leaders, we must communicate what their counter-parts in Europe and Japan have been doing as they also seek to solve the crisis of their cities. This is not an American problem only. And our overseas competitors already are ahead of us in some places.

## After Vision Comes Concept
The leader with vision to clearly see his objective, must have a **concept** — a conception of how to achieve it. HDP will help him focus his good ideas. The ideas, the solutions to problems must have realistic components. Concepts built on solid components may fit together only loosely at first, but that is the way the total package takes shape. A practical example or model of the concept is essential to attract financial support without which nothing happens.

To design such a concept, the developer must be aware of the modern methods and technologies available to him. He will rely not on conventional methods of the past, but the methods and technologies of today. The FTA now has embarked on a program to inform private developers of the new methods and technologies available to them.

## Then Comes Implementation
The developer then must **implement** the concept. This means applying modern business methods and techniques to get the job done. Implementation or building the concept is the last step in carrying the project through. HDP will guide the developer with check-points to follow. The best implementation is accomplished incrementally. It may require working with government, with business or both. It may require setting up new organizational structures. It will

inevitably require innovation in methodology, not just in technology. We have made an encouraging start on such innovative methodology. Results should be evident soon.

So we have three essentials: vision, concept and implementation.

There are many pitfalls, of course. Political pressures and procedures, broad freedom of action by all parties have led to poor performance in seeking mobility in our cities. Two of the biggest enemies of implementation are delay and compromise. Delay can double or triple costs. Compromise delivers something no one really wants or will use. And worse, a compromise consensus can fool an entire city into thinking something **good** is happening just because **something** is happening. That was the case in Pittsburgh when they abandoned the approved automated transit plan and retreated to something from the past. Detroit and Miami's downtown people movers also **did something**, but they ignored the market and failed.

But here is where leaders with vision must save the day. Such people will not be discouraged by those who fear innovation and want to fall back on the conventional solutions of the past. American business and industry gained world leadership through innovation. American business vision has given the U.S. the world's highest standard of living.

This is why I believe the future will find America providing world leadership in restoring people mobility and people activities to our cities. Europe and Japan have a lead on us in conventional public transportation. But we can capture world leadership in personal mobility if we harness the talents of our private architects, developers and other entrepreneurs who are driven by the profit incentive and where individual performance is rewarded.

U.S. entrepreneurs are looking for new business opportunities. They know all about how to build fixed costs into their budget structure. They know that providing mobility for their customers and potential customers can be handled as another cost of doing business. Providing mobility for people in our cities need not depend on great investment of public funds or subsidized fare structures. I ask again: when was the last time you had to pay a fare to ride a vertical elevator in a downtown high rise building?

The buzzword in government circles today is "privatization." But in transit, that has meant only letting the private entrepreneur — the developer — pay fees or taxes to support the conventional transportation for his potential customers.

I contend we must go to **real** privatization — call it "Private Privatization (PRP)." That means opening the way to private design, construction and operation of horizontally joined developments. Let the private entrepreneur do the whole job for his increment of a total network. Let him include the cost of moving people into and through his facility as part of his cost of doing business.

### How To Get the Private Developer Into The Act

If the private developers are so important to improving people mobility, how do we get them into the fray? The magic word is "profit." Not just a few percent profit, but excellent profit. Today private developers are quite confident that public transit is a loser. Just about everything they have ever read or heard says so. We have to prove to them that good profit can be made by building people mobility into their projects. Education and guidance is required with HDP before putting private developers in the political arena of conventional public transit.

One thing we don't have to teach anybody is that new transit service will increase land values. The transit industry and developers alike always have recognized that installing a new rail transit system raises real estate values around the stations and public transit developments.

An example is the Metro line built in Toronto in the late 1950s. A picture taken from a helicopter 10 years after the Jonge Street line was completed (see photo on page 130) shows the real estate development up Jonge Street extending in perpendicular spurs from three station stops. Although very little "horizontal planning" took place and the developments were entirely speculative, the land values increased significantly, ranging from 50 to 70 percent after five years.

That's the sort of thing a developer can understand. And we can project much greater gains when real horizontal planning is done and the old idea of isolated "stations" is eliminated.

Happily, we are starting to get some examples of such success. They demonstrate the economic feasibility of private developer investment in horizontal corridor transit increments. The FTA must get this information before other private developers and local officials in cities which are considering future development projects of major size. We must keep such development growing in our cities and avoid some of the suburban land sprawl and Edge City-itis.

I believe such evidence of success will ignite a wave of interest nationwide. There are more than 200 cities in America with high density areas ripe for this kind of solution.

*The appreciation of land values around rapid transit stations is demonstrated by three transit station developments along the Yonge Street subway in Toronto.*

**Table 1. Typical Land and Facilities Values for Toronto Transit Centers**

| Area | Sq. Ft. | Value Before Transit | Value 5 Yrs. After Transit | Increase After Transit | Cost of Developing Area | Value 5 Yrs. Later | Increase After Transit |
|------|---------|----------------------|----------------------------|------------------------|-------------------------|--------------------|------------------------|
| A | 200,000 | $ 400,000 | $ 1,600,000 | 4X | $10,000,000 | $17,000,000 | +70% |
| B | 2,000,000 | $ 4,000,000 | $ 12,000,000 | 3X | $40,000,000 | $68,000,000 | +70% |
| C | 25,000,000 | $50,000,000 | $100,000,000 | 2X | — | — | +50% |

Such change cannot be accomplished from the top down by a sweep of the political wand. The strategy must be to achieve change incrementally, just as Victor Gruen did when he established the first shopping mall, something which is now a permanent part of our life style. This change in approach must occur one location at a time, from city to city. Carried out well in the cities, it will soon by copied by the suburbs. John Portman's glass elevators and atrium design have spread throughout America in just a few years.

Trips from suburb to suburb now are twice as numerous as trips from suburb to center city. The incremental method of horizontal development, designed primarily for urban centers, will do even more for high density suburbs by bringing growth more into focus and enabling better land use.

The basic development approach is to intercept vehicles, including public mass transit, before they can enter and clog our downtown or high density areas. People then will be moved through the downtown by horizontal elevators which will take them right to the places they want to go. And with virtually no waiting. Although in the Lille system a transit vehicle comes every 55 seconds, most people wait only half that time. The average waiting time is 28 seconds since some walk directly into a waiting car. There is an 18 to 20 second "dwell time" at each stop.

To better understand how such a system of intercept and personal mobility is accomplished, look at figures 15A and 15B. In the first picture, you see the present growth process in our cities. Parking garages and lots are placed randomly with highways running right through some of the most valuable land. Large transit systems are designed to move people to the suburbs.

In the second picture, you see a strategic alternative, based on HDP, intercepting automobiles with mass transit lines at the perimeter of the downtown area. Horizontal elevators take the people from the intercept parking garages into the downtown center. Streets at the center will be for pedestrians only. As in Munich or Gothenburg, which was discussed in Chapter Eleven, they can be roofed over if desired to make room for people in the city center. The downtown can become a pleasant mall and the city merchants will once again make a profit.

This process is not "pie in the sky." It is being done now, incrementally. It can provide new life and new growth for our cities. HDP is the basic methodology to regain forward growth, even in high density areas.

We have the technology but we have to entice the bureaucracy to stand back and let the private sector go. Fortunately, on a small scale, the Federal Transit Administration (FTA), is now starting a small PRP investigation. Hopefully, it will demonstrate for the first time how to operate successfully the "multimodal" approach of Congress and the "privatization" of the Department of Transportation which has been touting the process for the past few years.

The big step has been to get FTA talking directly with private developers. If the public transit agencies and their consultants stay out of the picture at this point, they will benefit with major increases in patronage in the future.

In the past the so-called "comprehensive planning" process has meant assigning transit responsibilities to one group, construction and development to another and various other community responsibilities to a third or fourth. Then when each group has developed its plan, the plans are pulled together into a "comprehensive plan." Obviously, this system has not worked. Unified and integrated planning is urgently needed.

Some planning is partly a public process — such as closing streets in the city center to make room for people. But planning for people services and activities is a private function — the responsibility of business developers.

The Department of Transportation is receptive to working with private entrepreneurs to create the "enhanced mobility" they have been espousing for the past decade, but which has not yet happened.

We need our cities to be healthy, active and profitable. There is no limit to growth, only a limit to our knowledge of the **strategic methods** required for growth.

With vision in the planning process, knowledge of the methods and technologies available and an awareness of the successful mobility efforts being made elsewhere in the world, we can bring progress, excitement — and people — back to our urban centers.

Just imagine what can happen when leading architects and private developers are unleashed across the country. Their capacity for developing improved mobility is well beyond what FTA can achieve. There will be no need to fund the expensive projects for rail transit systems that require many years to build and pile up huge deficits. Just make certain the planning is carried out incrementally and integrated with development.

People today expect only low performance of public transit. They must be better informed about the great improvements possible and demand better transit performance in their cities. This is a communications challenge.

But the future is there for the taking. With vision in our planning and with the private developer in the center of the process, our cities can have double and triple the number of people enjoying freedom from traffic congestion. A new excitement and spirit will emerge in our cities. The Europeans and Japanese will again start to copy **us**.

If we do not exercise such vision, however, the outlook is grim. Federal processing will continue, deficits will grow larger, governments local, state and federal will be forced to ante up more and more funding only to see it go down the drain. Traffic congestion in our cities and major suburbs will get even worse than it is now.

Our hope for a new birth of public mobility lies with the resourcefulness of the private developers and their architects. They have a good track record. Let's give them the chance to help solve one of America's most critical problems.

# SUMMARY

W e have taken an excursion through the field of public mobility —
public and private ventures and investment that seek to improve
the mobility of people and reduce traffic congestion that is
choking our cities.

A summary of findings and recommendations is in order.

The public has invested billions of dollars in new transit systems such as BART
in San Francisco, MARTA in Atlanta and WMATA in Washington. These systems are operating well and are expanding. But their patronage is relatively poor
compared to Lille, France. Patronage falls short of the need. Traffic congestion
is getting worse instead of better. Annual subsidy requirements are increasing as
the transit agencies in these cities attempt to keep their systems viable for the
public.

The 10 public transit projects investigated at the request of the Congressional
Office of Technology Assessment (page 31) leave little doubt about the lack of
success. There has been no success in achieving even a reasonable ridership that
would impact traffic congestion and reach the government's goal of doubling
public transit use in the next decade.

*Clearly a major change in method is required.*
After years of investigation and study I am convinced that private increments of
**horizontally-developed** (HDP) automated transit systems offer the greatest
chance for achieving major improvement in public mobility in our high density city and its Edge, leading to a new growth process with profits replacing
deficits.

The Lille experience demonstrates that demand response is possible and that
riders can indeed be lured out of their automobiles for at least the most congested portion of their trip. Private developers believe that increases of from 10
to 15 percent in building occupancy rates and 8 to 12 percent in sales of large
retail businesses would easily justify their investing 3 to 5 percent of revenue in
horizontal elevator service to make these things happen.

The benefits would be real reductions in traffic congestion in high density areas along with increased capacity for growth in those urban and suburban centers. Reduced need for federal and state funds for public transit projects would save money for the taxpayer.

But some things must happen. . . **methods** must change.

Clearly these changes will not come from our present transit agencies who seem determined to maintain the status quo.

We finally are probing the potential of privatization in transit but the Federal Transit Administration must become knowledgeable about private developer processes and practices. The agency is now selecting several demonstration projects to sharpen the methodology. Some small private projects already exist in the U.S. and the city of Lille in France offers valid proof that the demand response for transit can be achieved in a large city.

We are about to spend $151 billion of ISTEA funds over the next six years on transportation programs. It is vital that we invest this huge sum much more intelligently than we did the $100 billion of the previous five years. It is vital, too, that we escape the hazards implicit in the increasing state control of a large portion of the funding. May the states resist the temptation to spend the money on supporting deficits, on just mending old systems or on pork barrel projects.

We are making probes into the promising world of private development. Let us hope that these private projects initiated by men and women of leadership and vision will show how to bring pleasure again to our cities and their edges. (Figs. 16A, 16B).

Perhaps the private developer will supply what is seriously lacking in our public mobility efforts today — a driving spirit to improve. The Romans had it in building their network of roads. The pioneering Americans had it in the early days of railroading. Even the trolley car builders had it in our cities many years ago. Today we are growing so fast that we appear to have lost the will to achieve new levels of performance required to attract and hold customers in public transit. Some people do not think it worthwhile or even possible to reach new levels of public mobility.

Lately there have been many serious articles questioning the lifeblood of our cities — usually projecting chaos or disasters beyond our ability to cope. Problems are described on massive terms implying the need for massive solutions. Somehow incremental improvement is never considered.

Such defeatism and lack of vision threatens the future of our cities. I am not one of those defeatists. I believe that there is a wonderful future ahead for our cities and suburban centers. I see great cities having long-term, continuing life. They have a way and a spirit which revitalizes them over and over again. All we need to do is apply with imagination and vision the methods and technology available to us. The problems cannot and need not be solved all at once. Small increments of improvement will grow and provide new paths. That's the secret of real "urban renewal." Take it one step at a time. The blueprint is there. In public mobility, the Horizontal Development Process is part of that blueprint. For the people in our cities, let's explore it.

# ACKNOWLEDGEMENTS

The seed for the central theme of this book probably was sown at the bottom of a 20,000 gallon electroplating tank in the spring of 1951 or 1952. I was down in that tank with the engineering manager of Oldsmobile, Don Burnham, studying how to keep impurities from reaching the automobile bumpers being electroplated. That where I started to learn about "methods improvement" — Don's specialty. His insistence on improved methods became my creed and that's what this book is all about: better methods in the field of public mobility. It has become clear to me that improving methods is really more important than improving technology, although you need both.

You can imagine my delight the day in 1954 when I learned that one Donald C. Burnham had been elected vice president of manufacturing for Westinghouse where he was to introduce so many new and improved manufacturing methods in that staid corporation which so badly needed the awakening. Under him, I continued my never-ending education in methods engineering and methods management.

When Westinghouse received the nation's first Urban Transportation Award, it was Don Burnham who handed me the award. It was for leadership in managing the development of new electric vehicles, development of the BART transit system, and creation of the world's first fully automated public transit system. Burnham became Chairman of Westinghouse, of course, and even to this day, 18 years after his retirement, he has continued to push me to get this book written and published.

The second person who has been pushing, and helping so much, is my wife Lee. She reads and corrects my correspondence and many of my writings. Without her untiring efforts to keep me going, and her support of my projects over the years, this work would never have been possible. It had to be frustrating for her. I once heard her tell a close friend: "George has written about some most interesting experiences, but he never has learned what a sentence is, and what it is not."

That's where Tom Phares comes in. Don Burnham had warned me not to try to write this book by myself. He told me I was a good engineer but no writer, and he advised me to get in touch with Tom, retired Westinghouse corporate communications manager. Tom and I got together, and after he rewrote the first couple of chapters, I never said another word about my writing ability.

Tom's work as writer, editor, and friend delivered much more to this project than I ever would have thought possible. Our association has been a very rewarding experience.

Many of my other former Westinghouse associates participated in the early work on this book, some knowingly, some without realizing it. They deserve to be acknowledged. That list includes: Phil Gillespie, marketing manager, Dixie Howell, project construction manager, Ray Marcum, transportation division manager in the 1960's, Ray Fields, Skybus project manager (deceased), Woody Johnson, transportation division manager in the 1970s and his manager of business development Tom Merrick.

Special mention should be made of the many meetings I held with the inventor of the Skybus fully-automated transit system concept, Charles Kerr, senior transportation engineer for Westinghouse (deceased).

When Westinghouse sold its transportation division to AEG of Germany, a whole new team was organized and they have been most helpful to me. Particularly so was Ken Fraelich, a young student engineer in the 1960s and today AEG's executive vice president for marketing and strategic business development. He read every page of this manuscript and made excellent corrections, principally correcting my memory. Ed Gordon, AEG manager of people mover marketing and Wendy Ruch, manager of communications, also have been most helpful.

Many people in far away places made lasting contributions to aid me in my work over the years, invaluable to the future of the HDP. Among them: Bob Fairborn, past president of the American Institute of Architects in Phoenix for his astute "cook book" analogy in expressing the need for something that would serve as a guide for the HDP; Tom Larson, supporter extraordinaire of HDP in his many transportation positions, private, state, and federal; Walter Heintzleman, transportation consultant, and Bob Anderson, highway consultant, both of whom reviewed the HDP work many times and provided excellent validation; Dr. Jim Palmer of George Mason University's regional mobility project of the FTA; Walter Kulyk, of FTA who has guided my work through many ups and downs in hope that the end result would be up.

There was Dave Bond, an architect (deceased) with whom I created Jernstedt-Bond Associates. Our marketing manager was Ed Ornsdorff, a former Westinghouse marketing friend. All of the above contributed to this book in some important way. To them my heartfelt thanks.

# COLOR PHOTO CREDITS

1 B : Atlanta News Agency

3 A, B, C, D : Seashore Trolley Museum

4 A, B : Westinghouse Electric Corp.

5 A, B, C, D : Hillsborough County
Aviation Authority

6 A, B : AEG Transportation Systems

7 A, B, C : Lille Metro Comeli

7 D : Eurolille Development

8 A : Bay Area Rapid
Transit District

8 B : Washington Area Metro
Transit Authority

8 C : MARTA Transit District

8 D : Metro-Dade Transit Agency

9 A, B : Otis Elevator Co.

9 C : VSL Corp.

9 D : Westinghouse Electric Corp.

12 A, B : AEG Transportation Systems

13 A, B : Hitachi

13 C : GEC Alsthom

14 A : Yamaman Real Estate
Development Co.

14 B : Kobe New Transit Co.

14 C : Otis Elevator Co.

14 D : AEG Transportation Systems

# TEXT REFERENCES

Although I have read several hundred books on the various phases of transportation and development, there have been virtually none written on the subject of public transit in the past 20 years. Literary agents report the opinion of publishers that there is no market for such books. People, they say, are not interested in reading about or riding on public transit. So this book is breaking new ground.

Excellent books on conventional transportation and horizontal development combined with real estate development are found in the library of the Urban Land Institute in Washington, D.C. I am sure material from the many texts I have read from this library has influenced some of my writings in assembling the Horizontal Development Process. I intend to continue to employ this fine resource in creative real estate writings.

Books on railroads are another story. There are two recent books on high speed trains. *Super Trains* by Joseph Vranich, 1991, St. Martins Press, New York City, and *Hi Tech Trains* by Arthur Taylor, 1992, Chartwell Book Inc., Secaucus, NJ. Unfortunately these interesting volumes do not address **how** high speed trains will relieve traffic congestion in our cities or how we can pay for such expensive facilities. This book attempts to bring new focus on how large increases in land values and new development opportunities can create markets and funding for public transit.

# I've Read the Book, Now What?

You've read the book, now what can you do to help improve public mobility in your community?

Making changes in public transit and development patterns in our country is a difficult process, but it can be done. Local planning organizations and transit agencies are responsible for maintaining public mobility as growth occurs or declines. So these organizations must be involved.

First, bring the problem to the attention of local business organizations which have a stake in community improvement, such as the Chamber of Commerce and business development associations. Likely locales for improvement will be those areas where density is increasing and traffic congestion is growing worse — sections of the city where people activities are declining.

You might start by sending copies of this book to key planners or business leaders and suggest they read it with your own community in mind. Point out the problem areas and urge action. Recommend presentations by knowledgable people in the development process, such as successful developers, architects, transit engineers. A gradual approach probably has the best chance of success. Attack the problem areas one at a time, with a total plan the ultimate goal.

The author has done this sort of thing in both the U.S. and abroad and is available to make presentations or participate in preliminary investigations of specific corridors which may respond to application of the Horizontal Development Process.

CITYSCOPE AND MOBILITY CO.
BOX 260 RD #1
BOLIVAR, PA 15923
Phones: (412) 238-2558
          (412) 235-2348
FAX:    (412) 235-2878

9347

ε